Raspberry PI
LCD
Projects

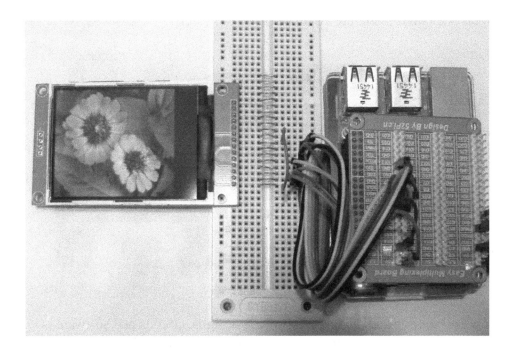

Robert J Davis II

Raspberry Pi LCD Projects
Copyright 2016 Robert j Davis II

A few years ago I wrote a book entitled "Arduino LCD Projects". I have been working on writing a similar LCD projects book for the Raspberry Pi for a while. However getting LCD's to work with the Raspberry Pi has not turned out to be that easy to do. There is no easy reference source, there are many varying standards, and there is required software that has numerous dependencies. In this book we will be using Python and the only dependency is that SPI be enabled.

I have a fairly large collection of LCD's to try to get to work with the Raspberry Pi. Eight of them, mostly on the left side in the next picture, are text based. The others are graphics based LCD's. Some of the graphics screens are serial, some are 8 bit and two of them are 16 bit devices.

As always building and using the following designs, circuits and software is solely the responsibility of the end user. Follow all safety rules; the safe operation of these devices is the responsibility of the reader. There is no warranty included or implied. If you are not familiar with using the Raspberry Pi and LCD's then start with something simpler like my LED projects book. Wiring mistakes can lead to a damaged Raspberry Pi or LCD screen.

Table of Contents.

Chapter 1

Raspberry Pi Setup

NOOBS

For this book we will be using NOOBS version 1.8 installed on an either an 8 or a 16 gig SD card. NOOBS 1.8 has a few more files than the older versions as you can see in the next picture.

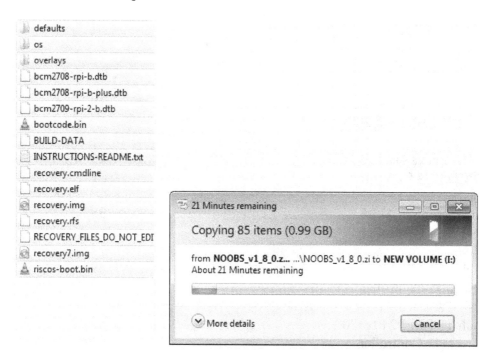

My Raspberry Pi accidentally lost power while it was setting up the NOOBS partitions and that rendered the SD card unusable. Microsoft Windows "Disk Management" could not fix the defective partitions. Then out of desperation I put the sick SD card in a camera and selected "format" on the camera. After formatting the SD card it could record on it. That trick actually worked and made the SD card usable again. I still had to format the SD card on the PC but it was back to a 16 Gig SD card.

Steps to install NOOBS:

1. Format the SD card
2. Un Zip the NOOBS files
3. Copy the files to the SD card.
4. Insert card in Raspberry Pi and power it on
5. Select "Install" and sit back and wait for a while

Raspberry Pi Model 2

For this book we will be using a Raspberry Pi model 2 B. However everything should still work on the Raspberry Pi model 1 but just a little bit slower. Besides being much faster, the model 2 B also has more GPIO pins as can be seen in the next picture. The left Raspberry Pi is a model 1A, and the right one is a model 2B. You might need a 26 pin header adapter to plug some things into the 2B because of the extra pins.

The Raspberry Pi model 2 is also a little bit more power hungry. A 1 amp AC adapter will work for a model 1, but model 2 should have at least 1.8 amps of power. There are some 1 amp adapters that can handle the Raspberry Pi model 2 but do not be surprised if it turns off on you!

The mounting holes also moved between the two models. There are now four mounting holes that are spaced 58mm or 2.28 inches by 49mm or 1.93 inches as can be seen in the next drawing. That means that any thing that uses the mounting holes will not be compatible with the newer version of the Raspberry Pi.

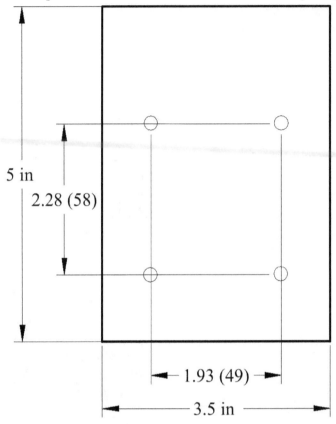

Raspberry Pi Zero

There is a smaller option that is available also, called the Raspberry Pi Zero. It was supposed to be a $5 single board computer. However they were quickly bought up and resold for $25 or more. With the introduction of the Pi Zero camera edition the price dropped under $20. However to use the Zero you will need to add a mini USB to regular USB adapter and or a hub. You will also need a Mini HDMI to regular HDMI adapter or cable.

This next picture shows the Raspberry Pi 1A, Raspberry Pi 2B and Raspberry Pi Zero from left to right.

Here is a picture of the three versions of the Raspberry Pi in their cases.

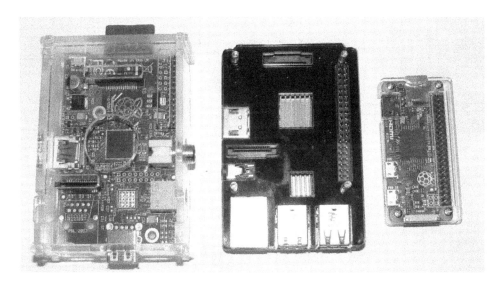

The case shown on the left easily snaps together. One of the corners broke off it when I tried to un-snap it. Also the hole for the GPIO connector does not fit the ribbon cable header. The middle case is for the PI 2B and consists of alternating layers of clear and black plastic. I am not crazy about it either, as it seems to reduce air flow and barely allows room for the heat sinks. One of the heat sinks was knocked off when I added the case. The Pi Zero case works nice but you will need to solder in some pins for the GPIO connector first if you plan on using the GPIO.

SPI

Some of the LCD displays we will examine in this book will use SPI to communicate with the LCD. Setting up the SPI interface has been greatly simplified in the newer software. Instead of having to modify a configuration file you can now just select SPI from "Menu", "Preferences" and "Raspberry Pi Configuration". Next you will need to click on "Interfaces" and "Enabled" next to SPI, then select "OK". After the raspberry Pi restarts SPI will then be enabled.

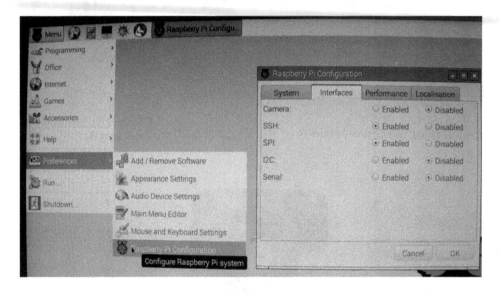

Chapter 2

Things to Make

GPIO Extender

If you want one, but do not have a GPIO extender then you can make one yourself. They charge way too much for these GPIO adapters. All you that need to have to make one for yourself is some header strips and some IC plugs that are designed to hold components. You will need a 26 pin IC component carrier, or you can also use a combination of two that adds up to the needed 26 pins.

Break off two sections of 13 pins each from the header strip. The short ends of the header strips are then bent out 90 degrees. Soldering the first row in place is the tricky part. The bent ends of the header strip will just barely reach the socket pins. Unfortunately they like to fall out of place when they are near their ends. The second row is easier to solder as the first row will keep them from falling out.

This next picture is the side view of the GPIO extender.

One way to solder the pins in place would be to plug the headers into a ribbon cable so that the cable connector would keep the headers aligned while they are being soldered into place.

This is the end view of the 26 pin GPIO header extender.

Logic Probe

You will likely need a working logic probe for troubleshooting some of the projects in this book. When I tried out my logic probe it apparently had died since that last time that I had used it. After taking it apart I decided that it was time to rebuild it. Here is how you can build your own logic probe or in my case rebuild a defective logic probe.

Basically what you need is a CMOS buffer to drive a "high" and "low" LED. Then you need a single shot that can detect a short pulse and extend it long enough so you can see it.

There is a capacitor that is located on the bottom side of the circuit board in this next picture. Also the pulse LED was too high so it had to be filed off so that it was shorter so it would fit inside of the cover.

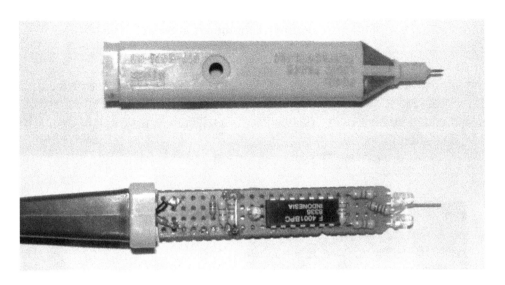

This is the schematic diagram of the logic probe design that I used. The "high" and "low" LED's normally go to a 1/2 the V+ voltage source. However that design does not make the LED's light bright enough for me. So by wiring the LED's to the power supply and ground instead, makes them much brighter. However with this design the LED's will also light very dimly even when there is no input.

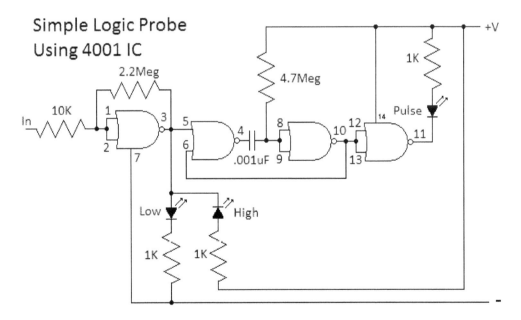

The +V power source can be anything from 3.3 volts to 12 volts. The 1K resistors can be 470 ohms if you want. The high and low LED's are normally red and green, the pulse LED is normally yellow in color. Some people add a 12 volt

Zener diode from the input to ground to protect the input as well as a 1N4001 diode in series with the V+ to protect the circuit from accidental power reversal.

Fitting the logic probe into the case was very tricky. Especially difficult is getting the input resistor lead to fit into the tip of the probe housing. Most of the time the resistors lead ended up bent over. Basically it is a trial and error thing to get the resistors lead to align properly.

Chapter 3

Adding Analog Inputs

Unlike the Arduino processors, the Raspberry Pi has no built in analog inputs. This can be cured by adding a MCP3008 (or MCP3208) eight port analog to digital converter. The MCP3008 can do 200,000 samples per second at 5 volts but we will be running it at 3.3 volts to keep the data input at the Raspberry Pi's 3.3 volts logic level.

Here is the schematic diagram and wiring chart for the MCP3008

```
CH0 ▭ 1        16 ▭ VDD
CH1 ▭ 2        15 ▭ VREF
CH2 ▭ 3        14 ▭ AGND
CH3 ▭ 4   MCP  13 ▭ CLK
CH4 ▭ 5   3008 12 ▭ DOUT-MISO
CH5 ▭ 6        11 ▭ DIN-MOSI
CH6 ▭ 7        10 ▭ CS
CH7 ▭ 8         9 ▭ DGND
```

MCP3008	Raspberry Pi Pin	Signal Name
1-8		Analog inputs 0 to 7
9	6	Gnd
10	24	CE0/8
11	19	MOSI/10
12	21	MISO/9
13	23	SCLK/11
14	6	Gnd
15	1	3.3V
16	1	3.3V

Up next is a schematic diagram of how to wire up the MCP3008.

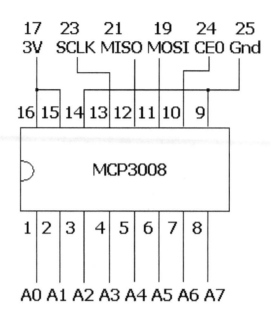

Here is a picture of a typical MCP3008 wiring arrangement. Some variable resistors were added for testing, they are the wires at the bottom of the picture. The wires at the top of the picture go to the Raspberry Pi I/O pins via a six conductor flexible cable.

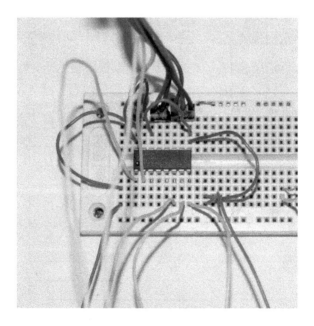

The MCP3008 communication protocol involves sending three 8 bit bytes. Going out from the Pi to the MCP3008, the first byte is mostly 0's but it ends in a "1" as a start bit. The next bit is a "1" if you are doing 8 analog converters as opposed to four double ended converters. The next three bits are the analog port selection bits. The remaining 12 bits do not matter as they are completely ignored.

Serial data starts coming back to the Raspberry Pi at bit 13 to bit 23 for a total of 10 bits. We need to check to see if the input is high or low after each clock then shift the results that are in "adcin" down one position to reconstruct the analog input value.

Here is the Python code to make it work. Direct access to the I/O lines is used because it is so much faster than when you are using SPI.

```
# MCP3008 communication
# Prints the contents of all 8 analog inputs.
import RPi.GPIO as GPIO
GPIO.setmode(GPIO.BCM)
GPIO.setup(8, GPIO.OUT)   # CE0
GPIO.setup(9, GPIO.IN)    # MISO
GPIO.setup(10, GPIO.OUT)  # MOSI
GPIO.setup(11, GPIO.OUT)  # Sclock

for port in range (0,8):
  GPIO.output(8, GPIO.HIGH) # deselect chip
  GPIO.output(11, GPIO.LOW) # set clock low
  adcin=0
  for shift in range (0,24): # 24 bits shifted
    GPIO.output(8, GPIO.LOW) # select chip
    GPIO.output(10, GPIO.LOW) # low for most bits
    if (shift==7 or shift==8):
        GPIO.output(10, GPIO.HIGH)
    if (shift==9)and(port > 3):
        GPIO.output(10, GPIO.HIGH)
    if (shift==10)and(port & 0x02):
        GPIO.output(10, GPIO.HIGH)
    if (shift==11)and(port & 0x01):
        GPIO.output(10, GPIO.HIGH)
    if (shift > 13)and(GPIO.input(9)):
        adcin = adcin+1 # set bit
    adcin = adcin << 1  # left shift 1
    GPIO.output(11, GPIO.LOW) # cycle the clock
    GPIO.output(11, GPIO.HIGH)
  print adcin
```

end

Analog Control Panel

Another thing that you might want to make is an analog input control panel.
Basically you mount from five to eight variable resistors on a panel and wire them
into the MCP3008 as its analog inputs. I had five multi turn variable resistors so I
used them for this project. They work great for the X and Y inputs for an Etch-a-
Sketch like display but they are not so good for selecting the color as it takes
several turns of the controls to select the color that you want to display.

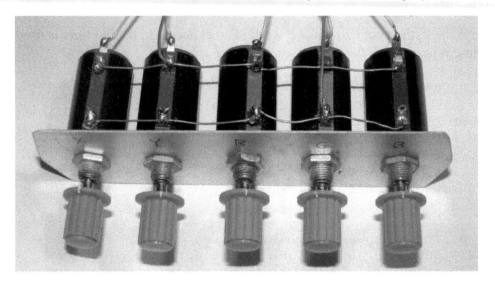

Here is the schematic diagram for the control panel.

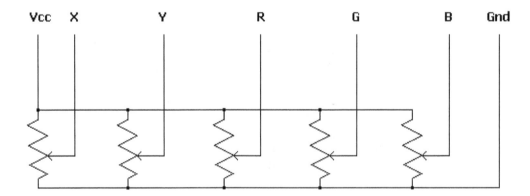

Alternate MCP3008 Setup

Some of the LCD screens will need to use the SPI pins to communicate with the Raspberry Pi. They cannot share the SPI with the MCP3008. To use the MCP3008 with a SPI screen you will need to change the pins and the software to match. This next wiring chart shows the new alternate arrangement to connect the MCP3008.

MCP3008	Raspberry Pi Pin	Signal Name
1-8		Analog inputs 0 to 7
9	6	Gnd
10	24 -> 11	CE0/8 -> 17
11	19 -> 13	MOSI/10 ->27
12	21 -> 12	MISO/9 ->18
13	23 ->15	SCLK/11 ->22
14	6	Gnd
15	1	3.3V
16	1	3.3V

The software to test the MCP3008 needs to be changed to match as follows.

```
# MCP3008 communication ALTERNATE pins
# Prints the contents of all 8 analog inputs.
import RPi.GPIO as GPIO

GPIO.setmode(GPIO.BCM)
GPIO.setup(17, GPIO.OUT)   # CE0
GPIO.setup(18, GPIO.IN)    # MISO
GPIO.setup(27, GPIO.OUT)  # MOSI
GPIO.setup(22, GPIO.OUT)  # Sclock

for port in range (0,8):
  GPIO.output(17, GPIO.HIGH) # deselect chip
  GPIO.output(22, GPIO.LOW) # set clock low
  adcin=0
  for shift in range (0,24): # 24 pits shifted
    GPIO.output(17, GPIO.LOW) # select chip
    GPIO.output(27, GPIO.LOW) # low for most bits
    if (shift==7 or shift==8):
      GPIO.output(27, GPIO.HIGH)
    if (shift==9)and(port & 0x04):
        GPIO.output(27, GPIO.HIGH)
    if (shift==10)and(port & 0x02):
```

```python
            GPIO.output(27, GPIO.HIGH)
        if (shift==11)and(port & 0x01):
            GPIO.output(27, GPIO.HIGH)
        if (shift > 13)and(GPIO.input(18)):
            adcin = adcin+1 # set bit
        adcin = adcin << 1  # left shift 1
        GPIO.output(22, GPIO.LOW) # cycle the clock
        GPIO.output(22, GPIO.HIGH)
    print adcin
GPIO.cleanup()
```

Chapter 4

Character Based LCD's

The first LCD project will be to get a text based 1602 or 2004 LCD working with the Raspberry Pi. The code for the 2004 will work just fine for the 1602 but the top two lines will be cut off at the first 16 characters. The bottom two lines will of course be missing all together.

For this project I am using a modified GPIO extension board. I changed the power connectors into sockets so they will work with any breadboard. Otherwise the power pins do not line up correctly with some breadboards.

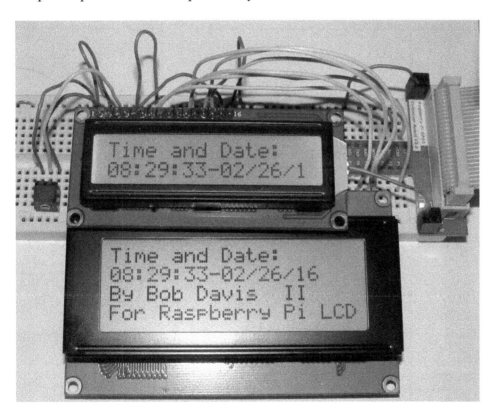

One of the problems with connecting a text based LCD to a Raspberry Pi is to figure out what arrangement is the "standard". Simply put - there is no real standard. Three of the more common configurations are the "AdaFruit", the "DVK512" and then there is what I call the "2004 demo" arrangement. Those are just some of the versions that use four data bits, to talk to the LCD display, there are also some arrangements that use eight data bits!

I chose to go with the 2004 demo design and software because it was a common arrangement and the software was easy to understand and to modify to my own likings. It was also easy to simplify the code to make it a lot shorter.

This next chart compares the connection arrangements of the three common arrangements. We will be using the 2004 demo arrangement.

LCD	2004 Demo	DVK512	Adafruit
1 - Ground	Pin 6/Gnd		
2 - Power	Pin 2/+5V		
3 - Potentiometer			
4 - RS	Pin26/GPIO7	Pin15/GPIO22	Pin22/GPIO25
5 - RW - Ground			
6 - EN	Pin24/GPIO8	Pin23/GPIO11	Pin18/GPIO24
7,8,9,10 - N.C.			
11 - D4	Pin22/GPIO25	Pin16/GPIO23	Pin16/GPIO23
12 - D5	Pin18/GPIO24	Pin19/GPIO10	Pin11/GPIO17
13 - D6	Pin16/GPIO23	Pin21/GPIO9	Pin13/GPIO21
14 - D7	Pin12/GPIO18	Pin22/GPIO25	Pin15/GPIO22
15 – LED + 5V			
16 - LED - Gnd			

The next picture is of the schematic diagram of how to wire the LCD to the Raspberry Pi. The variable resistor controls the contrast. It can be anything from 1K to 10K or even more. It is usually turned almost all of the way to one end to where the top row turns black when there is not data on the LCD. It can be fine tuned once the LCD is displaying text.

The LCD pin one is on the left and the Raspberry Pi pin one is on the right in the schematic.

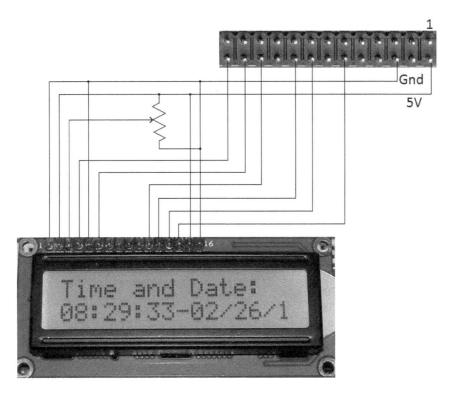

Here is the code to display the time on a 16 or 20 line LCD.

```
# HD44780 20x4/16x2 LCD time for Raspberry Pi
# Based on: Matt Hawkins @ raspberrypi-spy.co.uk
# Modified: Bob Davis
# Date     : 04/21/2016

# imports
import RPi.GPIO as GPIO
import time

# Define the GPIO to LCD mapping
LCD_RS = 7
LCD_E  = 8
LCD_D4 = 25
LCD_D5 = 24
LCD_D6 = 23
LCD_D7 = 18

# Define some device settings
LCD_WIDTH = 20 # Maximum characters
LCD_CHR = True
LCD_CMD = False
```

```python
# Timing delay
E_DELAY = 0.0001

def main():
  # Main program block
  GPIO.setmode(GPIO.BCM)   # Use BCM GPIO
  GPIO.setup(LCD_E, GPIO.OUT)  # E
  GPIO.setup(LCD_RS, GPIO.OUT) # RS
  GPIO.setup(LCD_D4, GPIO.OUT) # DB4
  GPIO.setup(LCD_D5, GPIO.OUT) # DB5
  GPIO.setup(LCD_D6, GPIO.OUT) # DB6
  GPIO.setup(LCD_D7, GPIO.OUT) # DB7

  # Initialise display
  lcd_init()
  #Convert time to a string
  times=time.strftime('%H:%M:%S-%D')

  # Send some test data, must have 20 characters
  lcd_byte(0x80, LCD_CMD)
  lcd_string("Time and Date:       ")
  lcd_byte(0xC0, LCD_CMD)
  lcd_string(times+"               ")
  lcd_byte(0x94, LCD_CMD)
  lcd_string("By Bob Davis  II     ")
  lcd_byte(0xD4, LCD_CMD)
  lcd_string("For Raspberry Pi LCD")

def lcd_init():
  # Initialise display
  lcd_byte(0x33,LCD_CMD) #Initialize
  lcd_byte(0x32,LCD_CMD) #Initialize
  lcd_byte(0x28,LCD_CMD) #data length num of lines
  lcd_byte(0x0c,LCD_CMD) #display on 0f=Cursor on
  lcd_byte(0x07,LCD_CMD) #move direction
  lcd_byte(0x01,LCD_CMD) #clear display

def lcd_string(message):
  for i in range(LCD_WIDTH):
    lcd_byte(ord(message[i]),LCD_CHR)

def lcd_byte(data, mode):
  # Send byte to data pins
  # mode  True=character, False=command
  GPIO.output(LCD_RS, mode) # RS
```

```
   # High bits
   GPIO.output(LCD_D4, data&0x10!=0)
   GPIO.output(LCD_D5, data&0x20!=0)
   GPIO.output(LCD_D6, data&0x40!=0)
   GPIO.output(LCD_D7, data&0x80!=0)

   # Toggle 'Enable' pin
   time.sleep(E_DELAY)
   GPIO.output(LCD_E, True)
   time.sleep(E_DELAY)
   GPIO.output(LCD_E, False)

   # Low bits
   GPIO.output(LCD_D4, data&0x01!=0)
   GPIO.output(LCD_D5, data&0x02!=0)
   GPIO.output(LCD_D6, data&0x04!=0)
   GPIO.output(LCD_D7, data&0x08!=0)

   # Toggle 'Enable' pin
   time.sleep(E_DELAY)
   GPIO.output(LCD_E, True)
   time.sleep(E_DELAY)
   GPIO.output(LCD_E, False)

if __name__ == '__main__':
  main()
```

If you wanted to display the value of an MCP3008 analog input you will need to add some more code to get it to work. There is a slight conflict as to the use of GPIO 8, pin 26 that might cause the display to come up blank intermittently. This coule be fixed by reassigning that pin.

```
# HD44780 20x4/16x2 LCD for Raspberry Pi
# Author  : Matt Hawkins-raspberrypi-spy.co.uk/
# Modified: by Bob Davis
# Date    : 04/21/2016

# imports
import RPi.GPIO as GPIO
import time
# Define GPIO to LCD mapping
LCD_RS = 7
LCD_E  = 8 #conflicts with MCP3008 CE
LCD_D4 = 25
LCD_D5 = 24
```

```
LCD_D6 = 23
LCD_D7 = 18
# Define some device constants
LCD_WIDTH = 20 # Maximum characters
# Timing constant
E_DELAY = 0.0001

# MCP3008 lines
GPIO.setmode(GPIO.BCM)    # Use BCM GPIO
GPIO.setup(8, GPIO.OUT)   # CE0
GPIO.setup(9, GPIO.IN)    # MISO
GPIO.setup(10, GPIO.OUT)  # MOSI
GPIO.setup(11, GPIO.OUT)  # Sclock
# LCD lines
GPIO.setup(LCD_E, GPIO.OUT)    # E
GPIO.setup(LCD_RS, GPIO.OUT)   # RS
GPIO.setup(LCD_D4, GPIO.OUT)   # DB4
GPIO.setup(LCD_D5, GPIO.OUT)   # DB5
GPIO.setup(LCD_D6, GPIO.OUT)   # DB6
GPIO.setup(LCD_D7, GPIO.OUT)   # DB7

def main():
  # Main program block
  # Initialise display
  lcd_init()
  # Send data must have <= 20 characters
  analogx=(readport(0)/4)
  analogy=(readport(1)/4)
  lcd_byte(0x80, 0)
  lcd_string("Analog 1 = "+str(analogx))
  lcd_byte(0xC0, 0)
  lcd_string("Analog 2 = "+str(analogy))
  lcd_byte(0x94, 0)
  lcd_string("Show Analog Inputs")
  lcd_byte(0xD4, 0)
  lcd_string("By Bob Davis II")

#Read the analog data
def readport(port):
  GPIO.output(8, GPIO.HIGH) # deselect chip
  GPIO.output(11, GPIO.LOW) # set clock low
  adcin=0
  for shift in range (0,24): # 24 pits shifted
    GPIO.output(8, GPIO.LOW) # select chip
    GPIO.output(10, GPIO.LOW) # low for most bits
    if (shift==7 or shift==8):
```

```python
      GPIO.output(10, GPIO.HIGH)
    if (shift==9)and(port & 0x04):
      GPIO.output(10, GPIO.HIGH)
    if (shift==10)and(port & 0x02):
      GPIO.output(10, GPIO.HIGH)
    if (shift==11)and(port & 0x01):
      GPIO.output(10, GPIO.HIGH)
    if (shift > 13)and(GPIO.input(9)):
      adcin = adcin+1 # set bit
    adcin = adcin << 1  # left shift 1
    GPIO.output(11, GPIO.LOW) # cycle the clock
    GPIO.output(11, GPIO.HIGH)
  return (adcin)

def lcd_init():
  # Initialise display
  lcd_byte(0x33,0) #Initialize
  lcd_byte(0x32,0) #Initialize
  lcd_byte(0x28,0) #data length num of lines
  lcd_byte(0x0c,0) #Display on, 0f=Cursor on
  lcd_byte(0x07,0) #move direction
  lcd_byte(0x01,0) #clear display

def lcd_string(message):
  # fix for lines shorter than 20 characters
  while (len(message) < LCD_WIDTH):
    message=(message+" ")
  for i in range(LCD_WIDTH):
    lcd_byte(ord(message[i]),1)

def lcd_byte(data, mode):
# The rest of the code is unchanged.
```

Chapter 5

Nokia Graphics 64x128

Nokia PCD8544 LCD's are low resolution Black and White LCD's. They are very inexpensive. Nevertheless they can be a lot of fun to play with. To display some text on a Nokia LCD you will need to design your own characters. Then you have to set up how they will be displayed on the screen. The picture below shows how to connect one to a Raspberry Pi.

This is a spreadsheet showing how to run the wires to the LCD.

LCD	Raspberry Pi
1 - Vcc	Pin 1
2 - Gnd	Pin 6
3 – SCE	Pin 24/GPIO8/CE0
4 – RST	Pin 18/GPIO24
5 – D/C	Pin 16/GPIO23
6 – DN (MODI)	Pin 19/GPIO10/MOSI
7 – SCLK	Pin 23/GPIO11/SCLK
8 - LED	10 ohms to Vcc

Here is the schematic diagram showing how to connect the Nokia display to the Raspberry pi. The LCD has pin 1 is on the left and the Raspberry Pi pin 1 is on the right, top side.

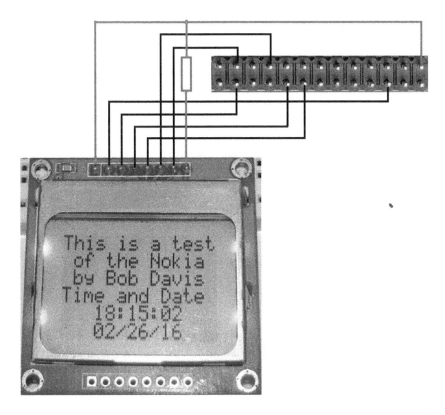

This is the code to display time and date on the Nokia display. It is simplified from code that was found on the internet. Support for RPi GPIO was also added.

```
# Nokia LCD Time test
# by Bob Davis
# Based on code found on Internet
# 5/5/2016

import time
import RPi.GPIO as GPIO
import spidev

contrast=0xc4
ROWS = 6
COLUMNS = 14
PIXELS_PER_ROW = 6
spi = spidev.SpiDev()

# gpio's :
DC   = 23 # gpio BCM pin 23
RST  = 24 # gpio BCM pin 24
# SPI connections
SCE  = 8  # gpio CE0 BCM 8)
SCLK = 11 # gpio SCLK BCM 11)
DIN  = 10 # gpio MOSI BCM 10)
CLSBUF=[0]*(ROWS * COLUMNS * PIXELS_PER_ROW)

font = {
  ' ': [0x00, 0x00, 0x00, 0x00, 0x00],
  '0': [0x3e, 0x51, 0x49, 0x45, 0x3e],
  '1': [0x00, 0x42, 0x7f, 0x40, 0x00],
  '2': [0x42, 0x61, 0x51, 0x49, 0x46],
  '3': [0x21, 0x41, 0x45, 0x4b, 0x31],
  '4': [0x18, 0x14, 0x12, 0x7f, 0x10],
  '5': [0x27, 0x45, 0x45, 0x45, 0x39],
  '6': [0x3c, 0x4a, 0x49, 0x49, 0x30],
  '7': [0x01, 0x71, 0x09, 0x05, 0x03],
  '8': [0x36, 0x49, 0x49, 0x49, 0x36],
  '9': [0x06, 0x49, 0x49, 0x29, 0x1e],
  'A': [0x7e, 0x11, 0x11, 0x11, 0x7e],
  'B': [0x7f, 0x49, 0x49, 0x49, 0x36],
  'C': [0x3e, 0x41, 0x41, 0x41, 0x22],
  'D': [0x7f, 0x41, 0x41, 0x22, 0x1c],
  'E': [0x7f, 0x49, 0x49, 0x49, 0x41],
  'F': [0x7f, 0x09, 0x09, 0x09, 0x01],
  'G': [0x3e, 0x41, 0x49, 0x49, 0x7a],
  'H': [0x7f, 0x08, 0x08, 0x08, 0x7f],
  'I': [0x00, 0x41, 0x7f, 0x41, 0x00],
  'J': [0x20, 0x40, 0x41, 0x3f, 0x01],
```

```
'K': [0x7f, 0x08, 0x14, 0x22, 0x41],
'L': [0x7f, 0x40, 0x40, 0x40, 0x40],
'M': [0x7f, 0x02, 0x0c, 0x02, 0x7f],
'N': [0x7f, 0x04, 0x08, 0x10, 0x7f],
'O': [0x3e, 0x41, 0x41, 0x41, 0x3e],
'P': [0x7f, 0x09, 0x09, 0x09, 0x06],
'Q': [0x3e, 0x41, 0x51, 0x21, 0x5e],
'R': [0x7f, 0x09, 0x19, 0x29, 0x46],
'S': [0x46, 0x49, 0x49, 0x49, 0x31],
'T': [0x01, 0x01, 0x7f, 0x01, 0x01],
'U': [0x3f, 0x40, 0x40, 0x40, 0x3f],
'V': [0x1f, 0x20, 0x40, 0x20, 0x1f],
'W': [0x3f, 0x40, 0x38, 0x40, 0x3f],
'X': [0x63, 0x14, 0x08, 0x14, 0x63],
'Y': [0x07, 0x08, 0x70, 0x08, 0x07],
'Z': [0x61, 0x51, 0x49, 0x45, 0x43],
'a': [0x20, 0x54, 0x54, 0x54, 0x78],
'b': [0x7f, 0x48, 0x44, 0x44, 0x38],
'c': [0x38, 0x44, 0x44, 0x44, 0x20],
'd': [0x38, 0x44, 0x44, 0x48, 0x7f],
'e': [0x38, 0x54, 0x54, 0x54, 0x18],
'f': [0x08, 0x7e, 0x09, 0x01, 0x02],
'g': [0x0c, 0x52, 0x52, 0x52, 0x3e],
'h': [0x7f, 0x08, 0x04, 0x04, 0x78],
'i': [0x00, 0x44, 0x7d, 0x40, 0x00],
'j': [0x20, 0x40, 0x44, 0x3d, 0x00],
'k': [0x7f, 0x10, 0x28, 0x44, 0x00],
'l': [0x00, 0x41, 0x7f, 0x40, 0x00],
'm': [0x7c, 0x04, 0x18, 0x04, 0x78],
'n': [0x7c, 0x08, 0x04, 0x04, 0x78],
'o': [0x38, 0x44, 0x44, 0x44, 0x38],
'p': [0x7c, 0x14, 0x14, 0x14, 0x08],
'q': [0x08, 0x14, 0x14, 0x18, 0x7c],
'r': [0x7c, 0x08, 0x04, 0x04, 0x08],
's': [0x48, 0x54, 0x54, 0x54, 0x20],
't': [0x04, 0x3f, 0x44, 0x40, 0x20],
'u': [0x3c, 0x40, 0x40, 0x20, 0x7c],
'v': [0x1c, 0x20, 0x40, 0x20, 0x1c],
'w': [0x3c, 0x40, 0x30, 0x40, 0x3c],
'x': [0x44, 0x28, 0x10, 0x28, 0x44],
'y': [0x0c, 0x50, 0x50, 0x50, 0x3c],
'z': [0x44, 0x64, 0x54, 0x4c, 0x44],
'{': [0x00, 0x08, 0x36, 0x41, 0x00],
'|': [0x00, 0x00, 0x7f, 0x00, 0x00],
'}': [0x00, 0x41, 0x36, 0x08, 0x00],
'~': [0x10, 0x08, 0x08, 0x10, 0x08],
```

```python
    "'": [0x00, 0x05, 0x03, 0x00, 0x00],
    '(': [0x00, 0x1c, 0x22, 0x41, 0x00],
    ')': [0x00, 0x41, 0x22, 0x1c, 0x00],
    '*': [0x14, 0x08, 0x3e, 0x08, 0x14],
    '+': [0x08, 0x08, 0x3e, 0x08, 0x08],
    ',': [0x00, 0x50, 0x30, 0x00, 0x00],
    '-': [0x08, 0x08, 0x08, 0x08, 0x08],
    '.': [0x00, 0x60, 0x60, 0x00, 0x00],
    '/': [0x20, 0x10, 0x08, 0x04, 0x02],
    ':': [0x00, 0x36, 0x36, 0x00, 0x00],
    ';': [0x00, 0x56, 0x36, 0x00, 0x00],
    '<': [0x08, 0x14, 0x22, 0x41, 0x00],
    '=': [0x14, 0x14, 0x14, 0x14, 0x14],
    '>': [0x00, 0x41, 0x22, 0x14, 0x08],
    '!': [0x00, 0x00, 0x5f, 0x00, 0x00],
    ',': [0x00, 0x50, 0x30, 0x00, 0x00],
    '-': [0x08, 0x08, 0x08, 0x08, 0x08],
    '.': [0x00, 0x60, 0x60, 0x00, 0x00],
    '?': [0x02, 0x01, 0x51, 0x09, 0x06],
    '`': [0x00, 0x01, 0x02, 0x04, 0x00],
    }
def setup():
  # Set pin directions.
  GPIO.setmode(GPIO.BCM)
  GPIO.setup(DC,GPIO.OUT)
  GPIO.setup(RST,GPIO.OUT)
  spi.open(0,0)
  spi.max_speed_hz=5000000

def gotoxy(x, y):
  GPIO.output(DC, False)
  spi.writebytes([x+128,y+64])

def cls():
  gotoxy(0, 0)
  GPIO.output(DC, True)
  spi.writebytes(CLSBUF)

def init():
  setup()
  # Toggle RST low to reset.
  GPIO.output(RST, False)
  time.sleep(0.100)
  GPIO.output(RST, True)
  # Extended mode, bias, vop, basic mode, non-inverted
display.
```

```
    GPIO.output(DC, False)
    spi.writebytes([0x21, 0x14, contrast, 0x20, 0x0c])

def text(string):
  for char in string:
    display_char(char)

def display_char(char):
  try:
    GPIO.output(DC, True)
    spi.writebytes(font[char]+[0])
  except KeyError:
    pass # Ignore undefined characters.

def main():
  init()
  cls()
  #Convert time and date to strings
  times=time.strftime('%H:%M:%S')
  dates=time.strftime('%D')
  text("This is a test of the Nokia  by Bob Davis Time and
Date:")
  text("    "+times)
  text("        "+dates)
  print 'Nokia LCD Updated'
  print

if __name__ == '__main__':
  main()
```

To display the values of an MCP3008 analog input ports you will need to add these lines near the top of the program. This uses the alternate arrangement of pins to not use the SPI pins.

```
# MCP3008 lines
GPIO.setmode(GPIO.BCM)
GPIO.setup(17, GPIO.OUT) # Replaces CE0
GPIO.setup(18, GPIO.IN)  # Replaces MISO
GPIO.setup(27, GPIO.OUT) # Replaces MOSI
GPIO.setup(22, GPIO.OUT) # Replaces Sclock
```

Then add this routine near the bottom.

```
def readport(port): # Alternate pins
  GPIO.output(17, GPIO.HIGH) # deselect chip
```

```
    GPIO.output(22, GPIO.LOW) # set clock low
    adcin=0
    for shift in range (0,24): # 24 pits shifted
      GPIO.output(17, GPIO.LOW) # select chip
      GPIO.output(27, GPIO.LOW) # low for most bits
      if (shift==7 or shift==8):
        GPIO.output(27, GPIO.HIGH)
      if (shift==9)and(port & 0x04):
        GPIO.output(27, GPIO.HIGH)
      if (shift==10)and(port & 0x02):
        GPIO.output(27, GPIO.HIGH)
      if (shift==11)and(port & 0x01):
        GPIO.output(27, GPIO.HIGH)
      if (shift > 13)and(GPIO.input(18)):
        adcin = adcin+1 # set bit
      adcin = adcin << 1  # left shift 1
      GPIO.output(22, GPIO.LOW) # cycle the clock
      GPIO.output(22, GPIO.HIGH)
    return (adcin)
```

Finally change the text lines in main() to look like this.

```
def main():
  init()
  cls()
  #Convert time and date to strings
  analog1=(readport(0))   # Range 0-1024
  analog2=(readport(1))
  analog3=(readport(2))
  analog4=(readport(3))
  times=time.strftime('%H:%M:%S')
  dates=time.strftime('%D')
  text(" Nokia Analog")
  gotoxy (0,1)
  text("by Bob DavisII")
  gotoxy (0,2)
  text("Analog 1 "+str(analog1))
  gotoxy (0,3)
  text("Analog 2 "+str(analog2))
  gotoxy (0,4)
  text("Analog 3 "+str(analog3))
  gotoxy (0,5)
  text("Analog 4 "+str(analog4))
  print 'Nokia LCD Updated'
  print
```

The next program will demonstrate some graphics being displayed instead of text. Displaying graphics on this screen is a little tricky. The data needs to be flipped around. The numbers that are right to left in the software will appear top to bottom on the screen. Each number controls 8 pixels once again going from top to bottom.

Here is the code to produce graphics on a Nokia LCD.

```
# Nokia LCD Graphics test
# by Bob Davis
# 5/5/2016

import time
import RPi.GPIO as GPIO
import spidev

contrast=0xc4
ROWS = 6
```

```
COLUMNS = 14
PIXELS_PER_ROW = 6
spi = spidev.SpiDev()

# gpio's :
DC   = 23 # gpio BCM 23
RST  = 24 # gpio BCM 24
# SPI connections
SCE  = 8  # gpio CE0 BCM 8)
SCLK = 11 # gpio SCLK BCM 11)
DIN  = 10 # gpio MOSI BCM 10)
CLSBUF=[0]*(ROWS * COLUMNS * PIXELS_PER_ROW)

image =[ # Left side top to bottom
  0x3e, 0x00, 0x00, 0x00, 0x00, 0x00, # First column
  0x41, 0x00, 0x00, 0x00, 0x00, 0x00,
  0x49, 0x00, 0x00, 0x00, 0x00, 0x00,
  0x49, 0x00, 0x00, 0x00, 0x00, 0x00,
  0x7a, 0x00, 0x00, 0x00, 0x00, 0x00,
  0x00, 0x00, 0x00, 0x00, 0x00, 0x00,
  0x7f, 0x00, 0x00, 0x00, 0xf0, 0x00,
  0x09, 0x00, 0x00, 0x00, 0xff, 0x00,
  0x19, 0x00, 0x00, 0xf0, 0xff, 0x00,
  0x29, 0x00, 0x00, 0xff, 0xff, 0x00, # 10th column
  0x46, 0x00, 0x00, 0xff, 0xff, 0x00,
  0x00, 0x00, 0x00, 0xff, 0xff, 0x00,
  0x7e, 0x00, 0xf0, 0xff, 0xff, 0x00,
  0x11, 0x00, 0xff, 0xff, 0xff, 0x00,
  0x11, 0xf0, 0x0f, 0xff, 0xff, 0x00,
  0x11, 0xf0, 0x00, 0xff, 0xff, 0x01,
  0x7e, 0x30, 0x00, 0xff, 0xff, 0x03,
  0x00, 0x30, 0x00, 0xff, 0xff, 0x07,
  0x7f, 0x30, 0x00, 0xff, 0xff, 0x0f,
  0x09, 0x30, 0x00, 0xff, 0xff, 0x1f, # 20th column
  0x09, 0x30, 0x00, 0xff, 0xff, 0x3f,
  0x09, 0x30, 0x00, 0xff, 0xff, 0x7f,
  0x06, 0x30, 0x00, 0xff, 0xff, 0x7f,
  0x00, 0x30, 0x00, 0xff, 0xff, 0x7f,
  0x7f, 0x30, 0x00, 0xff, 0xff, 0x7f,
  0x08, 0x30, 0x00, 0xff, 0xff, 0x7f,
  0x08, 0x30, 0x00, 0xff, 0xff, 0x7f,
  0x08, 0x30, 0x00, 0xff, 0xff, 0x3f,
  0x7f, 0x30, 0x00, 0xff, 0xff, 0x1f,
  0x00, 0x30, 0x00, 0xff, 0xff, 0x0f, # 30th column
  0x00, 0x30, 0x00, 0xff, 0xff, 0x07,
  0x41, 0x30, 0x00, 0xff, 0xff, 0x03,
```

```
0x7f, 0x30, 0x00, 0xff, 0xff, 0x01,
0x41, 0x30, 0x00, 0xff, 0xff, 0x00,
0x00, 0xf0, 0xff, 0xff, 0xff, 0x00,
0x00, 0xf0, 0xff, 0xff, 0xff, 0x00,
0x3e, 0x30, 0x00, 0xff, 0xff, 0x00,
0x41, 0x30, 0x00, 0xff, 0xff, 0x00,
0x41, 0x30, 0x00, 0xff, 0xff, 0x00,
0x41, 0x30, 0x00, 0xff, 0xff, 0x00, # 40th column
0x22, 0x30, 0x00, 0xff, 0xff, 0x00,
0x00, 0x30, 0x00, 0xff, 0xff, 0x00,
0x46, 0x30, 0x00, 0xff, 0xff, 0x00,
0x49, 0x30, 0x00, 0xff, 0xff, 0x00,
0x49, 0x30, 0x00, 0xff, 0xff, 0x00,
0x49, 0x30, 0x00, 0xff, 0xff, 0x00,
0x31, 0x30, 0x00, 0xff, 0xff, 0x00,
0x00, 0x30, 0x00, 0xff, 0xff, 0x00,
0x00, 0x30, 0x00, 0xff, 0xff, 0x00,
0x00, 0x30, 0x00, 0xff, 0xff, 0x00, # 50th column
0x00, 0x30, 0x00, 0xff, 0xff, 0x01,
0x00, 0x30, 0x00, 0xff, 0xff, 0x03,
0x00, 0x30, 0x00, 0xff, 0xff, 0x07,
0x01, 0x30, 0x00, 0xff, 0xff, 0x0f,
0x01, 0x30, 0x00, 0xff, 0xff, 0x1f,
0x7f, 0x30, 0x00, 0xff, 0xff, 0x3f,
0x01, 0xf0, 0x00, 0xff, 0xff, 0x7f,
0x01, 0xf0, 0x0f, 0xff, 0xff, 0x7f,
0x00, 0x00, 0xff, 0xff, 0xff, 0x7f,
0x7f, 0x00, 0xf0, 0xff, 0xff, 0x7f, # 60th column
0x49, 0x00, 0x00, 0xff, 0xff, 0x7f,
0x49, 0x00, 0x00, 0xff, 0xff, 0x7f,
0x49, 0x00, 0x00, 0xff, 0xff, 0x3f,
0x41, 0x00, 0x00, 0xff, 0xff, 0x1f,
0x00, 0x00, 0x00, 0xff, 0xff, 0x0f,
0x46, 0x00, 0x00, 0xff, 0xff, 0x07,
0x49, 0x00, 0x00, 0xff, 0xff, 0x03,
0x49, 0x00, 0x00, 0xff, 0xff, 0x01,
0x49, 0x00, 0x00, 0xff, 0xff, 0x00,
0x31, 0x00, 0x00, 0xff, 0xff, 0x00, # 70th column
0x00, 0x00, 0x00, 0xff, 0xff, 0x00,
0x01, 0x00, 0x00, 0xff, 0xff, 0x00,
0x01, 0x00, 0x00, 0xff, 0xff, 0x00,
0x7f, 0x00, 0x00, 0xff, 0xff, 0x00,
0x01, 0x00, 0x00, 0xff, 0xff, 0x00,
0x01, 0x00, 0x00, 0xff, 0xff, 0x00,
0x00, 0x00, 0x00, 0xff, 0xff, 0x00,
0x00, 0x00, 0x00, 0xf0, 0xff, 0x00,
```

```python
    0x00, 0x00, 0x00, 0x00, 0xff, 0x00,
    0x00, 0x00, 0x00, 0x00, 0xf0, 0x00, # 80th column
    0x00, 0x00, 0x00, 0x00, 0x00, 0x00,
    0x00, 0x00, 0x00, 0x00, 0x00, 0x00,
    0x5f, 0x00, 0x00, 0x00, 0x00, 0x00,
    0x5f, 0x00, 0x00, 0x00, 0x00, 0x00,
    0x00, 0x00, 0x00, 0x00, 0x00, 0x00
]

def setup():
  # Set pin directions.
  GPIO.setmode(GPIO.BCM)
  GPIO.setup(DC,GPIO.OUT)
  GPIO.setup(RST,GPIO.OUT)
  spi.open(0,0)
  spi.max_speed_hz=5000000

def gotoxy(x, y):
  GPIO.output(DC, False)
  spi.writebytes([x+128,y+64])

def cls():
  gotoxy(0, 0)
  GPIO.output(DC, True)
  spi.writebytes(CLSBUF)

def init():
  setup()
  # Toggle RST low to reset.
  GPIO.output(RST, False)
  time.sleep(0.100)
  GPIO.output(RST, True)
  # Extended mode, bias, vop, basic mode, non-inverted
display.
  GPIO.output(DC, False)
  spi.writebytes([0x21, 0x14, contrast, 0x20, 0x0c])

def lcd_data(value):
  GPIO.output(DC, True)
  spi.writebytes([value])

# Display image:
def load_image():
  gotoxy(0,0)
  for x in range(6): # Rop to bottom
    for y in range(84): # Left to Right
```

```python
            lcd_data(image[y*6+x])

def main():
    init()
    cls()
    load_image()
    print 'Nokia LCD Updated'
    print

if __name__ == '__main__':
    main()
```

Chapter 6

Mono Graphics 128x64

This next LCD is physically larger and has many more pixels than the Nokia display. It also has a lot more pins. These extra pins are because it is can accessed via a parallel connection instead of a serial connection. The controller chip that is used to run the LCD is the ST7920. Getting text to display on this LCD is actually very easy. The software for the text LCD's will actually run on this LCD display!

There are two minor changes that you need to make to the text program. First set the LCD_WIDTH = 16. The text lines are only 16 characters in length. Then change the vertical line positioning commands as follows:

```
# Send some data must have 16 characters
lcd_byte(0x80, 0)
lcd_string("Raspberry Pi LCD")
lcd_byte(0x90, 0)
lcd_string("128X64 Text Demo")
lcd_byte(0x88, 0)
lcd_string("By Bob Davis  II")
lcd_byte(0x98, 0)
lcd_string("1234567890123456")
```

Now if you want to make the text display even more interesting you can change the program to display some of the analog inputs from a MCP3008. First you need to add these lines to the beginning to set things up to read analog inputs.

```
# MCP3008 lines
GPIO.setmode(GPIO.BCM)
GPIO.setup(8, GPIO.OUT)  # CE0
GPIO.setup(9, GPIO.IN)   # MISO
GPIO.setup(10, GPIO.OUT) # MOSI
GPIO.setup(11, GPIO.OUT) # Sclock
```

Then add this routine among the other routines to do the job of reading the analog inputs.

```
#Read the analog data
def readport(port):
  GPIO.output(8, GPIO.HIGH) # deselect chip
  GPIO.output(11, GPIO.LOW) # set clock low
  adcin=0
  for shift in range (0,24): # 24 pits shifted
    GPIO.output(8, GPIO.LOW) # select chip
    GPIO.output(10, GPIO.LOW) # low for most bits
    if (shift==7 or shift==8):
      GPIO.output(10, GPIO.HIGH)
    if (shift==9)and(port & 0x04):
      GPIO.output(10, GPIO.HIGH)
    if (shift==10)and(port & 0x02):
      GPIO.output(10, GPIO.HIGH)
    if (shift==11)and(port & 0x01):
      GPIO.output(10, GPIO.HIGH)
    if (shift > 13)and(GPIO.input(9)):
      adcin = adcin+1 # set bit
    adcin = adcin << 1  # left shift 1
    GPIO.output(11, GPIO.LOW) # cycle the clock
    GPIO.output(11, GPIO.HIGH)
  return (adcin)
```

If the routine for sending data to the LCD does not pad the data then you will need to change it to pad the data to 16 characters.

```
def lcd_string(message):
  # fix for lines shorter than 16 characters
  while (len(message) < LCD_WIDTH):
    message=(message+" ")
  for i in range(LCD_WIDTH):
    lcd_byte(ord(message[i]),1)
```

Last of all change the text display lines to read and then display the analog inputs. Do not forget to keep the lines at 16 characters or less in length.

```
  # Send some data must have <= 16 characters
  analogx=(readport(0)/4)
  analogy=(readport(1)/4)
  lcd_byte(0x80, 0)
  lcd_string("Raspberry Pi LCD")
  lcd_byte(0x90, 0)
  lcd_string("By Bob Davis II ")
  lcd_byte(0x88, 0)
  lcd_string("Analog 1 = "+str(analogx))
  lcd_byte(0x98, 0)
  lcd_string("Analog 2 = "+str(analogy))
```

The bigger problem is getting this LCD display to do graphics images. Back when I used this LCD with the Arduino there were some issues in getting it to work right. For one thing you need to write data to the display only when the LCD is not busy. But because it is a five volt device the Raspberry Pi cannot safely read the status of the display. This results in garbage being displayed when the screen is being updated.

To switch this LCD into graphics mode first you have to enable the "extended instructions" by sending a 0x24 command. Then select graphics mode by sending a 0x26 command to the LCD. These bits are assigned as follows:

RS	RW	DB7	DB6	DB5	DB4	DB3	DB2	DB1	DB0
0	0	0	0	1	DL	x	RE	G	x

DL = 0 for 4 bit data transfers and DL = 1 for 8 bit transfers
RE = 0 for basic instructions and RE = 1 for extended instructions.
G = 0 for text and G = 1 for graphics

Next up is the new command to set the graphics display position:

RS	RW	DB7	DB6	DB5	DB4	DB3	DB2	DB1	DB0
0	0	1	AC6	AC5	AC4	AC3	AC2	AC1	AC0

This will set the GDRAM address coordinates to the address counter, AC. First you set the vertical address and then the horizontal address. This is done as two consecutive bytes to complete the vertical and horizontal address setup.

The vertical address range is AC6...AC0 (7 bits), the horizontal address range is AC3...AC0 (4 bits). Then you have to write a minimum of two bytes of data that will be sequentially displayed horizontally across the screen. The Address Counter (AC) will be increased by one after receiving these two 8 bit words of data for the next operation. The procedure to write some graphics to the LCD is summarized in these next steps:

1. Set vertical address (Y) for GDRAM (80 sets it to 0)
2. Set horizontal address (X) for GDRAM (80 sets it to 0)
3. Write D15~D8 to GDRAM (first byte of data)
4. Write D7~D0 to GDRAM (second byte of data)

5. Write additional data as desired until you reach the other side of the screen. Then go back and start over at step number one.

Coming up is the LCD's wiring chart. You might notice that the pinout is very similar to the pinout of the text only displays. The first 14 pins are exactly the same. There are just a few more pins additional pins that are involved. For instance PSB sets the display to serial mode if that is wanted.

LCD	Raspberry Pi	Definition
1 – Gnd	Pin 6	Gnd
2 – Vcc	Pin 2	5V
3 – Vo	Contrast Resistor	
4 - RS/CS	Pin26	GPIO7
5 - Read/Write	Gnd	
6 – Enable	Pin24	GPIO8
7 -10	NC	
11 - DB4	Pin22	GPIO25
12 - DB5	Pin18	GPIO24
13 - DB6	Pin16	GPIO23
14 - DB7	Pin12	GPIO18
15 – PSB	Pin 2	5V
16 – NC		
17 – Reset	Pin 2	5V
18 – NC		
19 – Vcc	Pin 2	5V
20 – Gnd	Pin 6	Gnd

The LCD's graphics mode worked best when the display is viewed sideways. That mode can yield up to 12 by 16 text characters. So to keep the programming simpler I went with a sideways display as you can see in the next picture.

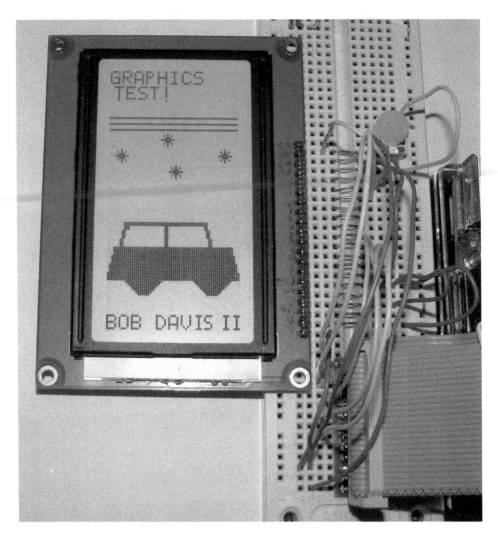

The next picture is the schematic diagram showing how to wire it up. Three of the additional pins are wired to five volts to disable the serial mode, etc.

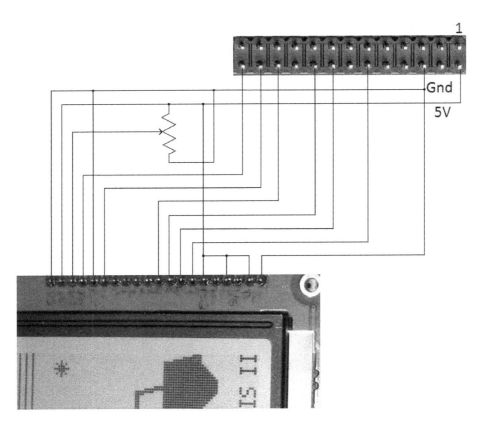

For displaying graphics you will need a lot of software. I reused the car graphics from the Nokia display but there was a lot of extra room above it so I added some stars and lines. The graphics programming makes more sense when it is displayed as lines of 16 bytes, but I cut the lines in half to better fit it in this book.

```
# ST7920 Graphics driver in python
# By Bob Davis
# 07/23/2016

import RPi.GPIO as GPIO
import time

# GPIO lines
LCD_RS=7
LCD_E =8
LCD_D4=25
LCD_D5=24
LCD_D6=23
LCD_D7=18
GPIO.setmode(GPIO.BCM)

# Define some device constants
```

```python
LCD_WIDTH = 16 # Maximum characters

# Timing constant
E_DELAY = 0.0005

# MCP3008 lines
GPIO.setup(8, GPIO.OUT)  # CE0
GPIO.setup(9, GPIO.IN)   # MISO
GPIO.setup(10, GPIO.OUT) # MOSI
GPIO.setup(11, GPIO.OUT) # Sclock

image =[ # Left side is 0
  0x7f, 0x00, 0x00, 0xf0, 0x00, 0x00, 0x00, 0x00, #Line1
  0x00, 0x00, 0x00, 0x00, 0x49, 0x00, 0x00, 0x3e,
  0x49, 0x00, 0x00, 0xff, 0x00, 0x00, 0x00, 0x00, #line2
  0x00, 0x00, 0x00, 0x00, 0x49, 0x00, 0x00, 0x41,
  0x49, 0x00, 0x00, 0xff, 0xf0, 0x00, 0x00, 0x00, #line3
  0x00, 0x00, 0x00, 0x00, 0x49, 0x00, 0x01, 0x49,
  0x49, 0x00, 0x00, 0xff, 0xff, 0x00, 0x00, 0x00, #line4
  0x00, 0x00, 0x08, 0x00, 0x49, 0x00, 0x01, 0x49,
  0x36, 0x00, 0x00, 0xff, 0xff, 0x00, 0x00, 0x00, #line5
  0x00, 0x00, 0x2a, 0x00, 0x49, 0x00, 0xff, 0x7a,
  0x00, 0x00, 0x00, 0xff, 0xff, 0x00, 0x00, 0x00, #line6
  0x00, 0x00, 0x1c, 0x00, 0x49, 0x00, 0x01, 0x00,
  0x3e, 0x00, 0x00, 0xff, 0xff, 0xf0, 0x00, 0x00, #line7
  0x00, 0x00, 0x7f, 0x00, 0x49, 0x00, 0x01, 0x7f,
  0x41, 0x00, 0x00, 0xff, 0xff, 0xff, 0x00, 0x00, #line8
  0x00, 0x00, 0x1c, 0x00, 0x49, 0x00, 0x00, 0x09,
  0x41, 0x00, 0x00, 0xff, 0xff, 0x0f, 0xf0, 0x00, #line9
  0x00, 0x00, 0x2a, 0x00, 0x49, 0x00, 0x7f, 0x19,
  0x41, 0x00, 0x01, 0xff, 0xff, 0x00, 0xf0, 0x00, #line10
  0x00, 0x00, 0x08, 0x00, 0x49, 0x00, 0x49, 0x29,
  0x3e, 0x00, 0x03, 0xff, 0xff, 0x00, 0xf0, 0x00, #line11
  0x00, 0x00, 0x00, 0x00, 0x49, 0x00, 0x49, 0x46,
  0x00, 0x00, 0x07, 0xff, 0xff, 0x00, 0x30, 0x00, #line12
  0x00, 0x00, 0x00, 0x00, 0x49, 0x00, 0x49, 0x00,
  0x7f, 0x00, 0x0f, 0xff, 0xff, 0x00, 0x30, 0x00, #line13
  0x00, 0x00, 0x00, 0x00, 0x49, 0x00, 0x41, 0x7e,
  0x49, 0x00, 0x1f, 0xff, 0xff, 0x00, 0x30, 0x00, #line14
  0x00, 0x00, 0x00, 0x00, 0x49, 0x00, 0x00, 0x11,
  0x49, 0x00, 0x3f, 0xff, 0xff, 0x00, 0x30, 0x00, #line15
  0x00, 0x00, 0x00, 0x00, 0x49, 0x00, 0x46, 0x11,
  0x49, 0x00, 0x7f, 0xff, 0xff, 0x00, 0x30, 0x00, #line16
  0x00, 0x00, 0x00, 0x00, 0x49, 0x00, 0x49, 0x11,
  0x36, 0x00, 0x7f, 0xff, 0xff, 0x00, 0x30, 0x00, #line17
  0x00, 0x00, 0x00, 0x00, 0x49, 0x00, 0x49, 0x7e,
  0x00, 0x00, 0x7f, 0xff, 0xff, 0x00, 0x30, 0x00, #line18
  0x00, 0x00, 0x00, 0x00, 0x49, 0x00, 0x49, 0x00,
  0x00, 0x00, 0x7f, 0xff, 0xff, 0x00, 0x30, 0x00, #line19
  0x00, 0x00, 0x00, 0x00, 0x49, 0x00, 0x31, 0x7f,
```

```
0x00, 0x00, 0x7f, 0xff, 0xff, 0x00, 0x30, 0x00, #line20
0x00, 0x00, 0x00, 0x00, 0x49, 0x00, 0x00, 0x09,
0x00, 0x00, 0x7f, 0xff, 0xff, 0x00, 0x30, 0x00, #line21
0x00, 0x00, 0x00, 0x00, 0x49, 0x00, 0x01, 0x09,
0x00, 0x00, 0x3f, 0xff, 0xff, 0x00, 0x30, 0x00, #line22
0x00, 0x00, 0x00, 0x00, 0x49, 0x00, 0x01, 0x06,
0x00, 0x00, 0x1f, 0xff, 0xff, 0x00, 0x30, 0x00, #line23
0x00, 0x00, 0x00, 0x00, 0x49, 0x00, 0x7f, 0x00,
0x00, 0x00, 0x0f, 0xff, 0xff, 0x00, 0x30, 0x00, #line24
0x00, 0x00, 0x00, 0x00, 0x49, 0x00, 0x01, 0x00,
0x7f, 0x00, 0x07, 0xff, 0xff, 0x00, 0x30, 0x00, #line25
0x00, 0x00, 0x00, 0x00, 0x49, 0x00, 0x01, 0x7f,
0x41, 0x00, 0x03, 0xff, 0xff, 0x00, 0x30, 0x00, #line26
0x00, 0x00, 0x00, 0x00, 0x49, 0x00, 0x00, 0x08,
0x41, 0x00, 0x01, 0xff, 0xff, 0x00, 0x30, 0x00, #line27
0x00, 0x00, 0x00, 0x08, 0x49, 0x00, 0x00, 0x08,
0x22, 0x00, 0x00, 0xff, 0xff, 0x00, 0x30, 0x00, #line28
0x00, 0x00, 0x00, 0x2a, 0x49, 0x00, 0x00, 0x08,
0x1c, 0x00, 0x00, 0xff, 0xff, 0xff, 0xf0, 0x00, #line29
0x00, 0x00, 0x00, 0x1c, 0x49, 0x00, 0x3f, 0x7f,
0x00, 0x00, 0x00, 0xff, 0xff, 0xff, 0xf0, 0x00, #line30
0x00, 0x00, 0x00, 0x7f, 0x49, 0x00, 0x00, 0x00,
0x7e, 0x00, 0x00, 0xff, 0xff, 0x00, 0x30, 0x00, #line31
0x00, 0x08, 0x00, 0x1c, 0x49, 0x00, 0x00, 0x00,
0x11, 0x00, 0x00, 0xff, 0xff, 0x00, 0x30, 0x00, #line32
0x00, 0x2a, 0x00, 0x2a, 0x49, 0x00, 0x00, 0x41, #Bottom
0x11, 0x00, 0x00, 0xff, 0xff, 0x00, 0x30, 0x00, #Line1
0x00, 0x1c, 0x00, 0x08, 0x49, 0x00, 0x00, 0x7f,
0x11, 0x00, 0x00, 0xff, 0xff, 0x00, 0x30, 0x00, #line2
0x00, 0x7f, 0x00, 0x00, 0x49, 0x00, 0x00, 0x41,
0x7e, 0x00, 0x00, 0xff, 0xff, 0x00, 0x30, 0x00, #line3
0x00, 0x1c, 0x00, 0x00, 0x49, 0x00, 0x00, 0x00,
0x00, 0x00, 0x00, 0xff, 0xff, 0x00, 0x30, 0x00, #line4
0x00, 0x2a, 0x00, 0x00, 0x49, 0x00, 0x00, 0x00,
0x1f, 0x00, 0x00, 0xff, 0xff, 0x00, 0x30, 0x00, #line5
0x00, 0x08, 0x00, 0x00, 0x49, 0x00, 0x00, 0x3e,
0x20, 0x00, 0x00, 0xff, 0xff, 0x00, 0x30, 0x00, #line6
0x00, 0x00, 0x00, 0x00, 0x49, 0x00, 0x00, 0x41,
0x40, 0x00, 0x00, 0xff, 0xff, 0x00, 0x30, 0x00, #line7
0x00, 0x00, 0x00, 0x00, 0x49, 0x00, 0x00, 0x41,
0x20, 0x00, 0x00, 0xff, 0xff, 0x00, 0x30, 0x00, #line8
0x00, 0x00, 0x00, 0x00, 0x49, 0x00, 0x00, 0x41,
0x1f, 0x00, 0x00, 0xff, 0xff, 0x00, 0x30, 0x00, #line9
0x00, 0x00, 0x00, 0x00, 0x49, 0x00, 0x00, 0x22,
0x00, 0x00, 0x00, 0xff, 0xff, 0x00, 0x30, 0x00, #line10
0x00, 0x00, 0x00, 0x00, 0x49, 0x00, 0x00, 0x00,
0x00, 0x00, 0x01, 0xff, 0xff, 0x00, 0x30, 0x00, #line11
0x00, 0x00, 0x00, 0x00, 0x49, 0x00, 0x00, 0x46,
0x41, 0x00, 0x03, 0xff, 0xff, 0x00, 0x30, 0x00, #line12
0x00, 0x00, 0x00, 0x00, 0x49, 0x00, 0x00, 0x49,
```

```
    0x7f, 0x00, 0x07, 0xff, 0xff, 0x00, 0x30, 0x00, #line13
    0x00, 0x00, 0x00, 0x00, 0x49, 0x00, 0x00, 0x49,
    0x41, 0x00, 0x0f, 0xff, 0xff, 0x00, 0x30, 0x00, #line14
    0x00, 0x00, 0x00, 0x00, 0x49, 0x00, 0x00, 0x49,
    0x00, 0x00, 0x1f, 0xff, 0xff, 0x00, 0x30, 0x00, #line15
    0x00, 0x00, 0x00, 0x00, 0x49, 0x00, 0x00, 0x31,
    0x46, 0x00, 0x3f, 0xff, 0xff, 0x00, 0xf0, 0x00, #line16
    0x00, 0x00, 0x00, 0x00, 0x49, 0x00, 0x00, 0x00,
    0x49, 0x00, 0x7f, 0xff, 0xff, 0x0f, 0xf0, 0x00, #line17
    0x00, 0x00, 0x00, 0x00, 0x49, 0x00, 0x00, 0x00,
    0x49, 0x00, 0x7f, 0xff, 0xff, 0xff, 0x00, 0x00, #line18
    0x00, 0x00, 0x00, 0x00, 0x49, 0x00, 0x00, 0x00,
    0x31, 0x00, 0x7f, 0xff, 0xff, 0xf0, 0x00, 0x00, #line19
    0x00, 0x00, 0x00, 0x00, 0x49, 0x00, 0x00, 0x00,
    0x00, 0x00, 0x7f, 0xff, 0xff, 0x00, 0x00, 0x00, #line20
    0x00, 0x00, 0x00, 0x00, 0x49, 0x00, 0x00, 0x00,
    0x00, 0x00, 0x7f, 0xff, 0xff, 0x00, 0x00, 0x00, #line21
    0x00, 0x00, 0x00, 0x00, 0x49, 0x00, 0x00, 0x00,
    0x00, 0x00, 0x7f, 0xff, 0xff, 0x00, 0x00, 0x00, #line22
    0x00, 0x00, 0x00, 0x00, 0x49, 0x00, 0x00, 0x00,
    0x00, 0x00, 0x3f, 0xff, 0xff, 0x00, 0x00, 0x00, #line23
    0x00, 0x00, 0x08, 0x00, 0x49, 0x00, 0x00, 0x00,
    0x00, 0x00, 0x1f, 0xff, 0xff, 0x00, 0x00, 0x00, #line24
    0x00, 0x00, 0x2a, 0x00, 0x49, 0x00, 0x00, 0x00,
    0x41, 0x00, 0x0f, 0xff, 0xff, 0x00, 0x00, 0x00, #line25
    0x00, 0x00, 0x1c, 0x00, 0x49, 0x00, 0x00, 0x00,
    0x7f, 0x00, 0x07, 0xff, 0xff, 0x00, 0x00, 0x00, #line26
    0x00, 0x00, 0x7f, 0x00, 0x49, 0x00, 0x00, 0x00,
    0x41, 0x00, 0x03, 0xff, 0xff, 0x00, 0x00, 0x00, #line27
    0x00, 0x00, 0x1c, 0x00, 0x49, 0x00, 0x00, 0x00,
    0x00, 0x00, 0x01, 0xff, 0xff, 0x00, 0x00, 0x00, #line28
    0x00, 0x00, 0x2a, 0x00, 0x49, 0x00, 0x00, 0x00,
    0x00, 0x00, 0x00, 0xff, 0xff, 0x00, 0x00, 0x00, #line29
    0x00, 0x00, 0x08, 0x00, 0x49, 0x00, 0x00, 0x00,
    0x41, 0x00, 0x00, 0xff, 0xf0, 0x00, 0x00, 0x00, #line30
    0x00, 0x00, 0x00, 0x00, 0x49, 0x00, 0x00, 0x00,
    0x7f, 0x00, 0x00, 0xff, 0x00, 0x00, 0x00, 0x00, #line31
    0x00, 0x00, 0x00, 0x00, 0x49, 0x00, 0x00, 0x00,
    0x41, 0x00, 0x00, 0xf0, 0x00, 0x00, 0x00, 0x00, #line32
    0x00, 0x00, 0x00, 0x00, 0x49, 0x00, 0x00, 0x00
    ]

def main():
    GPIO.setup (LCD_D4, GPIO.OUT)
    GPIO.setup (LCD_D5, GPIO.OUT)
    GPIO.setup (LCD_D6, GPIO.OUT)
    GPIO.setup (LCD_D7, GPIO.OUT)
    GPIO.setup (LCD_RS, GPIO.OUT)
    GPIO.setup (LCD_E, GPIO.OUT)
```

```python
  # Initialise display
  lcd_init()
  clear_screen()
  load_image()

# Clear graphics screen
def clear_screen():
  for y in range(0,32):
    lcd_byte(0x80+y,0) #Y=0
    lcd_byte(0x80,0) #X=0
    for x in range(0,32):
      lcd_byte(0x00,1)

# Display image:
def load_image():
  for y in range(0,32): # Y Top to bottom
    lcd_byte(0x80+y,0) #Y=0
    lcd_byte(0x80,0) #X=0
    for x in range(0,16): #X Left to Right top half
      lcd_byte(image[(y*16)+x],1)
    for x in range(0,16): #X Left to Right bottom half
      lcd_byte(image[(y*16)+512+x],1)

def lcd_init():  # Initialise display
  lcd_byte(0x33,0) #Initialize
  lcd_byte(0x32,0) #Initialize
  lcd_byte(0x28,0) #data length num of lines
  lcd_byte(0x0c,0) #Display on 0f=Cursor on
  lcd_byte(0x07,0) #move direction
  lcd_byte(0x01,0) #clear display

  lcd_byte(0x24,0) #Extended mode
  lcd_byte(0x26,0) #Graphics mode
  lcd_byte(0x80,0) #Y=0
  lcd_byte(0x80,0) #X=0

def lcd_byte(data, mode):
  # Send byte to data pins 1=data 0=command
  GPIO.output(LCD_RS, mode) # RS

 # High bits
  GPIO.output(LCD_D4, data&0x10!=0)
  GPIO.output(LCD_D5, data&0x20!=0)
  GPIO.output(LCD_D6, data&0x40!=0)
  GPIO.output(LCD_D7, data&0x80!=0)

  # Toggle 'Enable' pin
  time.sleep(E_DELAY)
  GPIO.output(LCD_E, True)
  time.sleep(E_DELAY)
```

```python
    GPIO.output(LCD_E, False)

    # Low bits
    GPIO.output(LCD_D4, data&0x01!=0)
    GPIO.output(LCD_D5, data&0x02!=0)
    GPIO.output(LCD_D6, data&0x04!=0)
    GPIO.output(LCD_D7, data&0x08!=0)

    # Toggle 'Enable' pin
    time.sleep(E_DELAY)
    GPIO.output(LCD_E, True)
    time.sleep(E_DELAY)
    GPIO.output(LCD_E, False)

if __name__ == '__main__':
    main()
#end
```

Chapter 7

1.8 Inch TFT SPI 128x160

This LCD supports color. But it takes a lot of code just to set up the screen. The LCD Built in controller is a ST7735. There are 16 commands that need to be sent to the controller and each command is followed by from 1 to 16 bytes of data that are the parameters for that command.

The code for this LCD found on the internet is wrong. It does not set it up properly. Also, if you change the LCD from using four or five bits per color (two bytes) to using six bits per color (three bytes) then the data will line up with the BMP file format. This makes displaying a BMP image very easy to do. Here is what the manual says about RGB mode06:

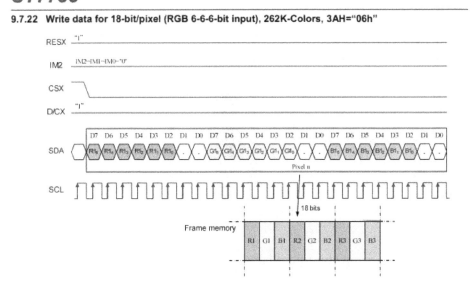

ST7735

9.7.22 Write data for 18-bit/pixel (RGB 6-6-6-bit input), 262K-Colors, 3AH="06h"

However displaying text is still a little difficult. The problem is that text is stored as data from the top to the bottom in columns and we are displaying text from left to right in rows. To fix this you will need to call up the text seven times, once for each horizontal row. Then depending upon what row you are on, you will need to mask out the bit that matches that row. Then you will need to send three bytes per bit/pixel. That way you will define the red, green and blue content for each bit. You could add a color parameter to the "text" command so you could specify the color as R, G, B, as it was done in the "fill" command.

Next up is the schematic diagram. For the resistor that powers the backlight I used a 10 ohm resistor. However, if there is a built in resistor so you could just use a jumper wire. Pin 1 of the LCD is on the left in the schematic and pin 1 of the Raspberry Pi is on the top right.

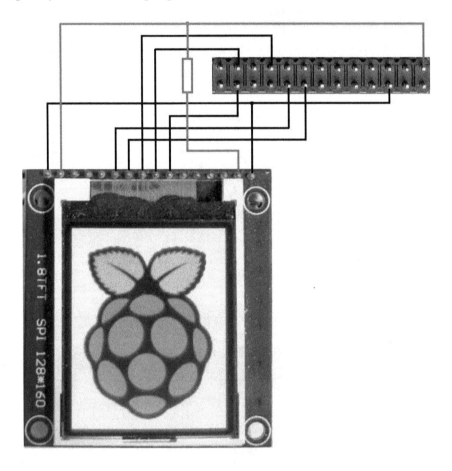

If you prefer to see a wiring chart here is one.

LCD	Raspberry Pi
1 – Gnd	Pin 6
2 - Vcc	Pin 1
3-5	NC

6 – RST	Pin 18/GPIO24
7 – A0 or D/C	Pin 16/GPIO23
8 – SDA or DIN	Pin 19/GPIO10/MOSI
9 – SCK	Pin 23/GPIO11/SCLK
10 – CS	Pin 24/GPIO8/CE0
11-14	NC
15 - LED	10 ohms to Vcc
16 - Gnd	Pin 6

This is a picture of the LCD wired up and working. My camera does not do a good job of showing how bright the colors are.

Here is the code to make it work. When you run the program the screen will produce some color stripes. The first stripe is red, then a green stripe, then a blue stripe. Then if the 128 by 128 bmp of "lena" is available it will be displayed. Next I created a 128 by 160 raspberry pi logo that it can display. Next it will do a color "etch a sketch" routine if you have a MCP3008 and five variable resistors attached to A0, A1 (X and Y) and A5 to A7 (Red, Green, Blue). Finally it will display some sample text that will include the status of the eight MCP3008 inputs if attached. The text is upsode down because of how the display is set up. The display can be inverted in the configuration files if needed.

```python
# ST7735 driver in python
# By Bob Davis
# Adapted from code on the Internet

import RPi.GPIO as GPIO
import spidev
import time
import sys

RS=23    # Data/Control Ao
RST=24   # Reset
SCE=8    # CS
SCLK=11  # SCLK Clock
DIN=10   # SDA MOSI
spi = spidev.SpiDev()

# MCP3008 ALTERNATE lines
GPIO.setmode(GPIO.BCM)
GPIO.setup(17, GPIO.OUT)  # Replaces CE0
GPIO.setup(18, GPIO.IN)   # Replaces MISO
GPIO.setup(27, GPIO.OUT)  # Replaces MOSI
GPIO.setup(22, GPIO.OUT)  # Replaces Sclock

font = { #Reduced font set UC and Numbers
   ' ': [0x00, 0x00, 0x00, 0x00, 0x00],
   '/': [0x20, 0x10, 0x08, 0x04, 0x02],
   '0': [0x3e, 0x51, 0x49, 0x45, 0x3e],
   '1': [0x00, 0x42, 0x7f, 0x40, 0x00],
   '2': [0x42, 0x61, 0x51, 0x49, 0x46],
   '3': [0x21, 0x41, 0x45, 0x4b, 0x31],
   '4': [0x18, 0x14, 0x12, 0x7f, 0x10],
   '5': [0x27, 0x45, 0x45, 0x45, 0x39],
   '6': [0x3c, 0x4a, 0x49, 0x49, 0x30],
   '7': [0x01, 0x71, 0x09, 0x05, 0x03],
   '8': [0x36, 0x49, 0x49, 0x49, 0x36],
```

```python
    '9': [0x06, 0x49, 0x49, 0x29, 0x1e],
    'A': [0x7e, 0x11, 0x11, 0x11, 0x7e],
    'B': [0x7f, 0x49, 0x49, 0x49, 0x36],
    'C': [0x3e, 0x41, 0x41, 0x41, 0x22],
    'D': [0x7f, 0x41, 0x41, 0x22, 0x1c],
    'E': [0x7f, 0x49, 0x49, 0x49, 0x41],
    'F': [0x7f, 0x09, 0x09, 0x09, 0x01],
    'G': [0x3e, 0x41, 0x49, 0x49, 0x7a],
    'H': [0x7f, 0x08, 0x08, 0x08, 0x7f],
    'I': [0x00, 0x41, 0x7f, 0x41, 0x00],
    'J': [0x20, 0x40, 0x41, 0x3f, 0x01],
    'K': [0x7f, 0x08, 0x14, 0x22, 0x41],
    'L': [0x7f, 0x40, 0x40, 0x40, 0x40],
    'M': [0x7f, 0x02, 0x0c, 0x02, 0x7f],
    'N': [0x7f, 0x04, 0x08, 0x10, 0x7f],
    'O': [0x3e, 0x41, 0x41, 0x41, 0x3e],
    'P': [0x7f, 0x09, 0x09, 0x09, 0x06],
    'Q': [0x3e, 0x41, 0x51, 0x21, 0x5e],
    'R': [0x7f, 0x09, 0x19, 0x29, 0x46],
    'S': [0x46, 0x49, 0x49, 0x49, 0x31],
    'T': [0x01, 0x01, 0x7f, 0x01, 0x01],
    'U': [0x3f, 0x40, 0x40, 0x40, 0x3f],
    'V': [0x1f, 0x20, 0x40, 0x20, 0x1f],
    'W': [0x3f, 0x40, 0x38, 0x40, 0x3f],
    'X': [0x63, 0x14, 0x08, 0x14, 0x63],
    'Y': [0x07, 0x08, 0x70, 0x08, 0x07],
    'Z': [0x61, 0x51, 0x49, 0x45, 0x43],
    '\\': [0x02, 0x04, 0x08, 0x10, 0x20],
    ':': [0x00, 0x36, 0x36, 0x00, 0x00],
}

def init():
  spi.open(0, 0)
  spi.max_speed_hz = 6000000
  GPIO.setmode(GPIO.BCM)
#  GPIO.setwarnings ( False )
  GPIO.setup (RS, GPIO.OUT)
  GPIO.setup (RST, GPIO.OUT)
  Reset()
  Write_cmd ( 0X11 )
  time.sleep ( 0.12 )
  Write_CD (( 0XB1, 0X01, 0X2C, 0X2D ))#Framerate
  Write_CD (( 0XB2, 0X01, 0X2C, 0X2D ))
  Write_CD (( 0XB3, 0X01, 0X2C, 0X2D, 0X01, 0X2C, 0X2D ))
  Write_CD (( 0XB4, 0X07 ))
  Write_CD (( 0XC0, 0XA2, 0X02, 0X84 ))#Power setup
```

```python
  Write_CD (( 0XC1, 0XC5 ))
  Write_CD (( 0XC2, 0X0A, 0X00 ))
  Write_CD (( 0XC3, 0X8A, 0X2A ))
  Write_CD (( 0XC4, 0X8A, 0XEE ))
  Write_CD (( 0XC5, 0X0E ))
  Write_CD (( 0X36, 0XC8 ))
  Write_CD (( 0XE0, 0X02, 0X1C, 0X07, 0X12, 0X37, 0X32,
0X29, 0X2D, 0X29, 0X25, 0X2B, 0X39, 0X00, 0X01, 0X03, 0X10
))
  Write_CD (( 0XE1, 0X03, 0X1D, 0X07, 0X06, 0X2E, 0X2C,
0X29, 0X2D, 0X2E, 0X2E, 0X37, 0X3F, 0X00, 0X00, 0X02, 0X10
))
  Write_CD (( 0X2A, 0X00, 0X00, 0X00, 0X79 ))
  Write_CD (( 0X2B, 0X00, 0X00, 0X00, 0X9f ))
  Write_CD (( 0X3A, 0X06 )) # Mode 06 is R G B
  Write_cmd ( 0X29 )

def Reset (): # Reset Display
  GPIO.output (RST, False )
  time.sleep ( 0.1 )
  GPIO.output (RST, True )
  time.sleep ( 0.1 )

def Write_cmd (cmd): # Write Command
  GPIO.output (RS, False )  # RS = 0
  spi.writebytes([cmd])

def Write_data (Data): # Write data
  GPIO.output (RS, True )   # RS = 1
  spi.writebytes([Data])

def Write_CD (cmd): #Write command followed by data
  if len (cmd) == 0 :
    return
  GPIO.output (RS, False ) # RS = 0
  spi.writebytes ([cmd [ 0 ]])
  GPIO.output (RS, True )  # RS = 1
  spi.writebytes ( list (cmd [ 1 :]))

def Fill (red, green, blue):
  Write_cmd ( 0X2C ) # Next: red, Green, Blue bytes
  GPIO.output (RS, True )  # RS = 1
  pixline = []
  for n in range (384): # Fill screen with white
    if (blue==1):pixline.append (0xff) # Blue
    else :pixline.append (0x00) # Blue
```

```python
      if (green==1):pixline.append (0xff) # Green
      else :pixline.append (0x00) # Green
      if (red==1):pixline.append (0xff) # RED
      else: pixline.append (0x00) # RED
   for n in range (128):   # send data to LCD
      spi.writebytes (pixline [ 0 :])


def goto (x,y):  # go to top/bottom
      Write_CD (( 0X2A, 0X00, x, 0X00, 0X7f  ))
      Write_CD (( 0X2B, 0X00, y, 0X00, 0x9f ))
      Write_cmd ( 0X2C ) # Next: red, Green, Blue bytes
      GPIO.output (RS, True )  # RS = 1 will send data


def Image (filename):
#  GPIO.output ( RS, True ) # RS = 1
   try:  # Prevents crashing when images do not work
      with open(filename, 'rb') as bitmap: # Must be 128
        for x in range ( 168 ):
          pixline = []
          for y in range ( 384 ):
            bitmap.seek(0x36 + x*384 + y) # 36 is header
            Pixel = ord(bitmap.read(1))
            pixline.append (Pixel)
          spi.writebytes (pixline)
   except:
      pass


def text(string, red, green, blue):
   string=string.ljust(21, " ")
   for row in range(10): # 8 rows top to bottom
     pixline = []
     for char in string: # Procees each character in string
       for byte in range(5):
         data=(font[char])  # Load 5 bytes of character
         pix=0
         if (row==0) and (data[byte] & 0x01):pix=1
         if (row==1) and (data[byte] & 0x02):pix=1
         if (row==2) and (data[byte] & 0x04):pix=1
         if (row==3) and (data[byte] & 0x08):pix=1
         if (row==4) and (data[byte] & 0x10):pix=1
         if (row==5) and (data[byte] & 0x20):pix=1
         if (row==6) and (data[byte] & 0x40):pix=1
         if (row==7) and (data[byte] & 0x80):pix=1
         if (row==8):pix=0  # Blank between lines
         if (row==9):pix=0  # Blank between lines
         if (pix==1):        # fill in R/G/B
```

```python
        if (blue==1): pixline.append (0xff)
        else: pixline.append (0x00)
        if (green==1): pixline.append (0xff)
        else: pixline.append (0x00)
        if (red==1):  pixline.append (0xff)
        else: pixline.append (0x00)
      else:
          pixline.append (0x00)
          pixline.append (0x00)
          pixline.append (0x00)
    pixline.append (0x00) # blanks btw characters
    pixline.append (0x00)
    pixline.append (0x00)
  for filler in range(6):  # Add 2 blank lines
    pixline.append (0x00) # 6x21=126+2=128
  spi.writebytes(pixline)
  pixline = []

def readport(port): # Alternate pins
  GPIO.output(17, GPIO.HIGH) # deselect chip
  GPIO.output(22, GPIO.LOW) # set clock low
  adcin=0
  for shift in range (0,24): # 24 pits shifted
    GPIO.output(17, GPIO.LOW) # select chip
    GPIO.output(27, GPIO.LOW) # low for most bits
    if (shift==7 or shift==8):
      GPIO.output(27, GPIO.HIGH)
    if (shift==9)and(port & 0x04):
      GPIO.output(27, GPIO.HIGH)
    if (shift==10)and(port & 0x02):
      GPIO.output(27, GPIO.HIGH)
    if (shift==11)and(port & 0x01):
      GPIO.output(27, GPIO.HIGH)
    if (shift > 13)and(GPIO.input(18)):
      adcin = adcin+1 # set bit
    adcin = adcin << 1  # left shift 1
    GPIO.output(22, GPIO.LOW) # cycle the clock
    GPIO.output(22, GPIO.HIGH)
  return (adcin)

def sketch():
  for y in range(0,10000):
    pixline=[]
    analogx=(readport(0)/8)
    analogy=(readport(1)/8)
    analogr=(readport(5)/4)
```

```
        analogg=(readport(6)/4)
        analogb=(readport(7)/4)
        if analogx>128:analogx=128
        if analogy>128:analogy=128
        goto (analogx, analogy)
        # Next: RGB bytes
        pixline.append (analogr)
        pixline.append (analogg)
        pixline.append (analogb)
        spi.writebytes(pixline)
    time.sleep(.01)

if __name__ == "__main__" :
    init ()
    T1 = time.clock ()
    goto(0,32)
    Fill (1,0,0) # Red
    goto(0,64)
    Fill (0,1,0) # Green
    goto(0,96)
    Fill (0,0,1) # Blue
    goto(0,128)
    Fill (1,1,1) # white
    time.sleep(2)
    goto(0,0)
    Image ("lena.bmp")
    time.sleep(2)
    goto(0,0)
    Image ("RPI-128.bmp")
    time.sleep(2)
    Fill (0,0,0) # black
    sketch()

    #Convert time and date to strings
    times=time.strftime('%H:%M:%S')
    dates=time.strftime('%D')
    # Read analog ports
    analog1=(readport(0))   # Range 0-1024
    analog2=(readport(1))
    analog3=(readport(2))
    analog4=(readport(3))
    analog5=(readport(4))   # Range 0-1024
    analog6=(readport(5))
    analog7=(readport(6))
    analog8=(readport(7))
    goto(0,0)
```

57

```
text("THIS IS A LCD TEST", 1,0,0) # Red
text("BY BOB DAVIS II", 0,1,0)  # green
text("TIME AND DATE", 0,0,1) # Blue
text(times+" "+dates, 1,1,1)     # white
text("ANALOG 1 IS "+str(analog1),1,1,1)
text("ANALOG 2 IS "+str(analog2),1,1,0)
text("ANALOG 3 IS "+str(analog3),0,1,1)
text("ANALOG 4 IS "+str(analog4),1,0,1)
text("ANALOG 5 IS "+str(analog5),1,1,1)
text("ANALOG 6 IS "+str(analog6),1,1,0)
text("ANALOG 7 IS "+str(analog7),0,1,1)
text("ANALOG 8 IS "+str(analog8),1,0,1)

T2 = time.clock ()
print 'Processing Time:' , str (T2 - T1)
```

Chapter 8

2.8 Inch TFT SPI 240x320

The next LCD is also a serial SPI interfaced device. The connections are different, in fact they are reversed (pin 1 is on the right) and the code to run the LCD is also different. This LCD comes in various sizes ranging from 2 inches up to 2.8 inches measured diagonally. Also the software driver was improved to include double sized text and to flip the images horizontally so they are displayed correctly.

This is a wiring chart – note that Vcc and Gnd (ground) are reversed from the previous LCD's. You only need seven wires to send data to this LCD. The LED pin eight can be jumpered directly to pin one. I like to use a resistor just in case there is not one already included in the display. Don't forget that pin 1 is on the right side this time.

LCD	Raspberry Pi
1 – Vcc	Pin 1 (3.3V)
2 - Gnd	Pin 6
3 - CS	Pin 24/GPIO8/CE0
4 – RST	Pin 18/GPIO24
5 – D/C	Pin 16/GPIO23
6 – SDI/MOSI	Pin 19/GPIO10/MOSI
7 – SCK	Pin 23/GPIO11/SCLK
8 – LED	10 ohms to Vcc
9 – SDO/MISO	NC
10-14	NC

Coming up next is a picture of the LCD set up. Unlike the previous LCD's, Pin one of the LCD and the Raspberry Pi are both located on the right.

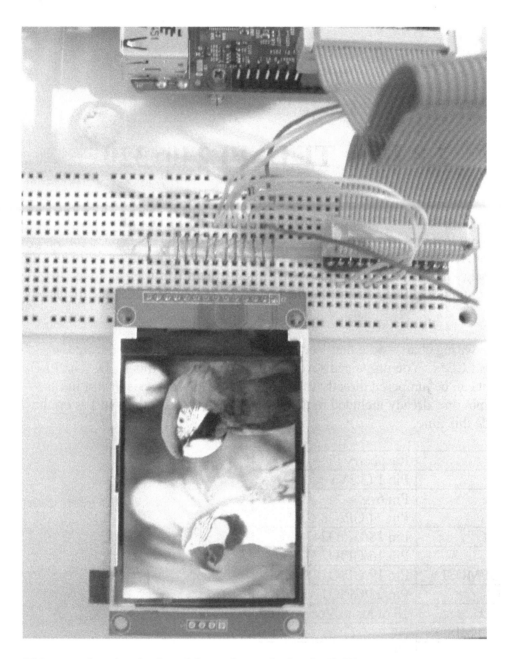

This next drawing is the wiring schematic for the LCD.

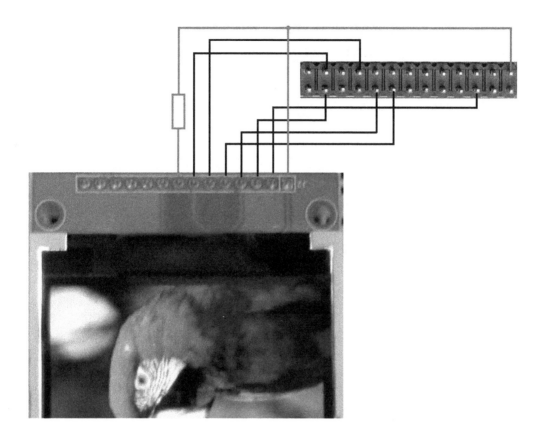

Once again the normal settings for this LCD need to be modified for the RGB mode that is used by BMP files. Command 3A needs to be set to 06.

8.2.33. COLMOD: Pixel Format Set (3Ah)

3Ah	PIXSET (Pixel Format Set)											
	D/CX	RDX	WRX	D17-8	D7	D6	D5	D4	D3	D2	D1	D0	HEX
Command	0	1	↑	XX	0	0	1	1	1	0	1	0	3Ah
Parameter	1	1	↑	XX	0	DPI [2:0]			0	DBI [2:0]			66
Description	This command sets the pixel format for the RGB image data used by the interface. DPI [2:0] is the pixel format select of RGB interface and DBI [2:0] is the pixel format of MCU interface. If a particular interface, either RGB interface or MCU interface, is not used then the corresponding bits in the parameter are ignored. The pixel format is shown in the table below.											

DPI [2:0]			RGB Interface Format
0	0	0	Reserved
0	0	1	Reserved
0	1	0	Reserved
0	1	1	Reserved
1	0	0	Reserved
1	0	1	16 bits / pixel
1	1	0	18 bits / pixel
1	1	1	Reserved

DBI [2:0]			MCU Interface Format
0	0	0	Reserved
0	0	1	Reserved
0	1	0	Reserved
0	1	1	Reserved
1	0	0	Reserved
1	0	1	16 bits / pixel
1	1	0	18 bits / pixel
1	1	1	Reserved

If using RGB Interface must selection serial interface.

X = Don't care

This is the code for the ILI9341 driver and demonstration program. I added the ability to select larger text called "dtext" by making the text twice as wide and twice as tall. The demo pictures are modified with IrfanView by taking images and then converting them to be 240 pixels wide BMP's. It also reads the contents of the MCP3008 and displays them as well as uses them for a color sketch demo.

I did not list the entire font file as it is available on the Internet and elsewhere in this book. Also the image is being reversed right to left so that the image is correctly displayed on the LCD by using "720-y" instead of just using "y".

```
# ILI9341 driver in python
# By Bob Davis
# Adapted from code on the Internet

import RPi.GPIO as GPIO
import spidev
import time
import sys

RS=23    # Data/Control Ao
RST=24   # Reset
SCE=8    # CS
SCLK=11  # SCLK Clock
DIN=10   # SDA MOSI
spi = spidev.SpiDev()

# MCP3008 ALTERNATE lines
GPIO.setmode(GPIO.BCM)
GPIO.setup(17, GPIO.OUT) # Replaces CE0
GPIO.setup(18, GPIO.IN)  # Replaces MISO
GPIO.setup(27, GPIO.OUT) # Replaces MOSI
GPIO.setup(22, GPIO.OUT) # Replaces Sclock

font = {  # Reduced Character Set
   ' ': [0x00, 0x00, 0x00, 0x00, 0x00],
   '/': [0x20, 0x10, 0x08, 0x04, 0x02],
   '0': [0x3e, 0x51, 0x49, 0x45, 0x3e],
   '1': [0x00, 0x42, 0x7f, 0x40, 0x00],
   '2': [0x42, 0x61, 0x51, 0x49, 0x46],
   '3': [0x21, 0x41, 0x45, 0x4b, 0x31],
   '4': [0x18, 0x14, 0x12, 0x7f, 0x10],
   '5': [0x27, 0x45, 0x45, 0x45, 0x39],
   '6': [0x3c, 0x4a, 0x49, 0x49, 0x30],
   '7': [0x01, 0x71, 0x09, 0x05, 0x03],
   '8': [0x36, 0x49, 0x49, 0x49, 0x36],
```

```python
    '9': [0x06, 0x49, 0x49, 0x29, 0x1e],
    ':': [0x00, 0x36, 0x36, 0x00, 0x00],
    '=': [0x14, 0x14, 0x14, 0x14, 0x14],
    'A': [0x7e, 0x11, 0x11, 0x11, 0x7e],
    'B': [0x7f, 0x49, 0x49, 0x49, 0x36],
    'C': [0x3e, 0x41, 0x41, 0x41, 0x22],
    'D': [0x7f, 0x41, 0x41, 0x22, 0x1c],
    'E': [0x7f, 0x49, 0x49, 0x49, 0x41],
    'F': [0x7f, 0x09, 0x09, 0x09, 0x01],
    'G': [0x3e, 0x41, 0x49, 0x49, 0x7a],
    'H': [0x7f, 0x08, 0x08, 0x08, 0x7f],
    'I': [0x00, 0x41, 0x7f, 0x41, 0x00],
    'J': [0x20, 0x40, 0x41, 0x3f, 0x01],
    'K': [0x7f, 0x08, 0x14, 0x22, 0x41],
    'L': [0x7f, 0x40, 0x40, 0x40, 0x40],
    'M': [0x7f, 0x02, 0x0c, 0x02, 0x7f],
    'N': [0x7f, 0x04, 0x08, 0x10, 0x7f],
    'O': [0x3e, 0x41, 0x41, 0x41, 0x3e],
    'P': [0x7f, 0x09, 0x09, 0x09, 0x06],
    'Q': [0x3e, 0x41, 0x51, 0x21, 0x5e],
    'R': [0x7f, 0x09, 0x19, 0x29, 0x46],
    'S': [0x46, 0x49, 0x49, 0x49, 0x31],
    'T': [0x01, 0x01, 0x7f, 0x01, 0x01],
    'U': [0x3f, 0x40, 0x40, 0x40, 0x3f],
    'V': [0x1f, 0x20, 0x40, 0x20, 0x1f],
    'W': [0x3f, 0x40, 0x38, 0x40, 0x3f],
    'X': [0x63, 0x14, 0x08, 0x14, 0x63],
    'Y': [0x07, 0x08, 0x70, 0x08, 0x07],
    'Z': [0x61, 0x51, 0x49, 0x45, 0x43],
    '\\': [0x02, 0x04, 0x08, 0x10, 0x20],
}

def init():
  spi.open(0, 0)
  spi.max_speed_hz = 60000000  # Maximum safe speed.
  GPIO.setmode(GPIO.BCM)
#  GPIO.setwarnings ( False )
  GPIO.setup (RS, GPIO.OUT)
  GPIO.setup (RST, GPIO.OUT)
  Reset()
  Write_cmd ( 0X11 )
  time.sleep ( 0.12 )
# RPI ILI9341 driver
  Write_CD((0xCF, 0x00, 0X83, 0X30))
  Write_CD((0xED, 0x64, 0x03, 0X12, 0X81) )
  Write_CD((0xE8, 0x85, 0x01, 0x79))
```

```python
      Write_CD((0xCB, 0x39, 0x2C, 0x00, 0x34, 0x02) )
      Write_CD((0xF7, 0x20))
      Write_CD((0xEA, 0x00, 0x00))
      Write_CD((0xC0, 0x26)) # Power control
      Write_CD((0xC1, 0x11)) # Power control
      Write_CD((0xC5, 0x35, 0x3e)) # VCM control
      Write_CD((0xC7, 0xbe)) # VCM control2
      Write_CD((0x36, 0x48)) # 40=RGB Memory Control
      Write_CD((0x3A, 0x06)) # Sequential r,g,b bytes
      Write_CD((0xB1, 0x00, 0x1b))
      Write_CD((0xB6, 0x0a, 0x82, 0x27, 0x00))# Display
      Write_CD((0xF2, 0x00)) # 3Gamma Function Disable
      Write_CD((0x26, 0x01)) # Gamma curve selected
      Write_CD((0xE0, 0x0F, 0x31, 0x2B, 0x0C, 0x0E, 0x08, 0x4E,
0xF1, 0x37, 0x07, 0x10, 0x03, 0x0E, 0x09, 0x00))
      Write_CD((0xE1, 0x00, 0x0E, 0x14, 0x03, 0x11, 0x07, 0x31,
0xC1, 0x48, 0x08, 0x0F, 0x0C, 0x31, 0x36, 0x0F))
      Write_cmd(0x29)        # Display on
      Write_CD (( 0X2A, 0X00, 0X00, 0X00, 0XEf )) #240 Col
      Write_CD (( 0X2B, 0X00, 0X00, 0X01, 0X3F )) #320 row
      Write_cmd ( 0X2C ) # Next: red, Green, Blue bytes

def Reset (): # Reset Display
  GPIO.output (RST, False )
  time.sleep ( 0.1 )
  GPIO.output (RST, True )
  time.sleep ( 0.1 )
def Write_cmd (cmd): # Write Command
  GPIO.output (RS, False )  # RS = 0
  spi.writebytes([cmd])
def Write_data (Data): # Write data
  GPIO.output (RS, True )   # RS = 1
  spi.writebytes([Data])
def Write_CD (cmd): #Write command followed by data
  if len (cmd) == 0 :
    return
  GPIO.output (RS, False ) # RS = 0
  spi.writebytes ([cmd [ 0 ]])
  GPIO.output (RS, True )  # RS = 1
  spi.writebytes ( list (cmd [ 1 :]))

def Fill (red, green, blue):
  pixline = []
  for n in range (0,320): # Fill screen with white
    if (blue==1):pixline.append (0xff) # Blue
    else :pixline.append (0x00) # Blue
```

```
      if (green==1):pixline.append (0xff) # Green
      else :pixline.append (0x00) # Green
      if (red==1):pixline.append (0xff) # RED
      else: pixline.append (0x00) # RED
    for n in range (240):   # send data to LCD
      spi.writebytes (pixline [ 0 :])

def goto (x, y):  # go to x y coordinates
  if (y>255): # Fix for numbers over 255
    Y = y-256
    Write_CD (( 0X2A, 0X00, x, 0X00, 0XEf )) #240 Col
    Write_CD (( 0X2B, 1, y, 0X01, 0X3F )) #320 rows
  else:
    Write_CD (( 0X2A, 0X00, x, 0X00, 0XEf )) #240 Col
    Write_CD (( 0X2B, 0X00, y, 0X01, 0X3F )) #320 rows
  Write_cmd ( 0X2C ) # Next: red, Green, Blue bytes
  GPIO.output (RS, True )  # RS = 1 will send data

def Image (filename):
  try:  # Prevents crashing when images do not work
    with open(filename, 'rb') as bitmap: # Must be 128x128
image
      for x in range ( 0,320 ):
        pixline = []
        for y in range ( 0,720 ):
          bitmap.seek(0x36 + x*720 + (719-y)) # 36 is
header size
          Pixel = ord(bitmap.read(1)) # 719-y reverse image
horizontally
          pixline.append (Pixel)
        spi.writebytes (pixline)
  except:
      pass

def text(string, red, green, blue):
  if (red==1):red=255
  if (green==1):green=255
  if (blue==1):blue=255
  string=string.ljust(40, " ") # 240/6=40 characters
  for row in range(0,10): # 10 rows top to bottom
    pixline = []
    for char in string: # Procees each character in string
      for byte in range(0,5):
        data=(font[char])  # Load 5 bytes of character
        pix=0
        if (row<8):
```

```
          if(data[byte]>>row & 0x01):pix=1
        if (row>7):pix=0  # Blank between lines
        if (pix==1):        # fill in R/G/B
          pixline.append (blue)
          pixline.append (green)
          pixline.append (red)
        else:
          pixline.append (0x00)
          pixline.append (0x00)
          pixline.append (0x00)
      pixline.append (0x00) # blanks between characters
      pixline.append (0x00)
      pixline.append (0x00)
    spi.writebytes(pixline)
    pixline = []

def dtext(string, red, green, blue): # double size text
  if (red==1):red=255
  if (green==1):green=255
  if (blue==1):blue=255
  string=string.ljust(20, " ") # 240/6=40 characters
  for row in range(0,20): # 20 rows top to bottom
    pixline = []
    for char in string: # Procees each character in string
      for byte in range(0,5):
        data=(font[char])  # Load 5 bytes of character
        pix=0
        if (row<17):
          if(data[byte]>>(row/2) & 0x01):pix=1
        if (row>16):pix=0  # Blank between lines
        for twice in range(0,2):
          if (pix==1):        # fill in R/G/B
            pixline.append (blue)
            pixline.append (green)
            pixline.append (red)
          else:
            pixline.append (0x00)
            pixline.append (0x00)
            pixline.append (0x00)
      for i in range(0,6):
        pixline.append (0x00) # blanks between characters
    spi.writebytes(pixline)
    pixline = []

def readport(port): # Alternate pins
  GPIO.output(17, GPIO.HIGH) # deselect chip
```

```python
  GPIO.output(22, GPIO.LOW) # set clock low
  adcin=0
  for shift in range (0,24): # 24 pits shifted
    GPIO.output(17, GPIO.LOW) # select chip
    GPIO.output(27, GPIO.LOW) # low for most bits
    if (shift==7 or shift==8):
      GPIO.output(27, GPIO.HIGH)
    if (shift==9)and(port & 0x04):
      GPIO.output(27, GPIO.HIGH)
    if (shift==10)and(port & 0x02):
      GPIO.output(27, GPIO.HIGH)
    if (shift==11)and(port & 0x01):
      GPIO.output(27, GPIO.HIGH)
    if (shift > 13)and(GPIO.input(18)):
      adcin = adcin+1 # set bit
    adcin = adcin << 1  # left shift 1
    GPIO.output(22, GPIO.LOW) # cycle the clock
    GPIO.output(22, GPIO.HIGH)
  return (adcin)

def sketch():
  for y in range(0,10000):
    pixline=[]
    analogx=(readport(0)/4)
    analogy=(readport(1)/3)
    analogr=(readport(5)/4)
    analogg=(readport(6)/4)
    analogb=(readport(7)/4)
    goto (analogx, analogy)
    # Next: RGB bytes
    pixline.append (analogr)
    pixline.append (analogg)
    pixline.append (analogb)
    spi.writebytes(pixline)
  time.sleep(.01)

if __name__ == "__main__" :
  init ()
  T1 = time.clock ()
  goto (0, 64)
  Fill (1,0,0) # Blue
  goto (0, 128)
  Fill (0,1,0) # Green
  goto (0, 192)
  Fill (0,0,1) # Red
  goto (0, 256)
```

```
Fill (1,1,1) # white
time.sleep(2)
goto(0,0)
Image ("RPI-240.bmp")
time.sleep(2)
goto(0,0)
Image ("Parrots-240.bmp")
time.sleep(2)
Fill (0,0,0) # black
sketch()
time.sleep(2)
goto(0,0)
Fill (0,0,0) # black
#Convert time and date to strings
times=time.strftime('%H:%M:%S')
dates=time.strftime('%D')
# Read analog ports
analog1=(readport(0))   # Range 0-1024
analog2=(readport(1))
analog3=(readport(2))
analog4=(readport(3))
analog5=(readport(4))
analog6=(readport(5))
analog7=(readport(6))
analog8=(readport(7))
text("THIS IS A TEST OF THE 320X240 LCD", 1,0,0) # Blue
text("WRITTEN BY ROBERT J DAVIS II", 0,1,0)  # green
text("THE CURRENT DATE AND TIME IS:", 0,0,1) # RED
text(times+" "+dates, 1,1,1)     # white
dtext ("IN BIGGER LETTERS:", 1,0,1)
dtext(times+" "+dates, 1,1,1)     # white
text("ANALOG 1 IS "+str(analog1),1,1,1)
text("ANALOG 2 IS "+str(analog2),1,1,0)
text("ANALOG 3 IS "+str(analog3),0,1,1)
text("ANALOG 4 IS "+str(analog4),1,0,1)
text("ANALOG 5 IS "+str(analog5),1,1,1)
text("ANALOG 6 IS "+str(analog6),1,1,0)
text("ANALOG 7 IS "+str(analog7),0,1,1)
text("ANALOG 8 IS "+str(analog8),1,0,1)
T2 = time.clock ()
print 'Processing Time:' , str (T2 - T1)
```

Chapter 9

2.4 Inch TFT Parallel 240x320

Adapting a parallel LCD is a little tricky as there are no parallel ports available on the Raspberry Pi like there is on the Arduino. What has to be done is each 8 bit byte is broken down to bits and then the output pin matching the bit is set. Another problem is that the data comes in 16 bits but we are only sending 8 bits at a time. So the data needs to be shifted so that the correct 8 bits is sent.

This software can run at least two different LCD's. The one in back of the next picture that is wired up via jumper wires on a breadboard is the HY TFT 240. In the foreground the 2.4 TFT 240x320 V2.1 has an adapter so that it can plug directly into the ribbon cable. The pinout of the two LCD's are very similar. However the closer LCD has two rows of pins making it difficult to plug it into the breadboard.

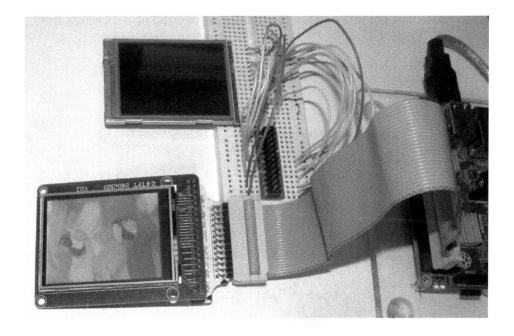

To plug in both the ribbon cable to the LCD and the analog to digital converter you can use something like the multi I/O adapter such as the one in the next picture.

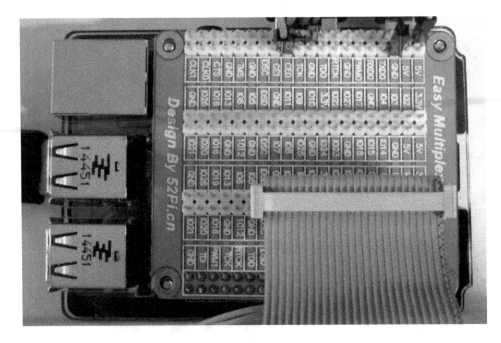

This next picture shows how some of the LCD's have almost identical pin assignments. Note that the one LCD at the bottom is inverted or backwards from all of the other LCD's.

This is a wiring chart if you are not using an adapter.

LCD pins	Raspberry Pi Pins	Pi Pin Name
Gnd	6	Gnd
VCC	2	+5V
NC		
RS	5	SCL
RW	3	SDA
RD	1	+3V (Disabled)
DB8	11	GPIO0
DB9	12	GPIO1
DB10	13	GPIO2
DB11	15	GPIO3
DB12	16	GPIO4
DB13	18	GPIO5
DB14	22	GPIO6
DB15	7	GPIO7
CS	26	CE1
NC		
RST	10	RX
NC		

This is the schematic diagram if you are manually wiring it up instead of using an adapter.

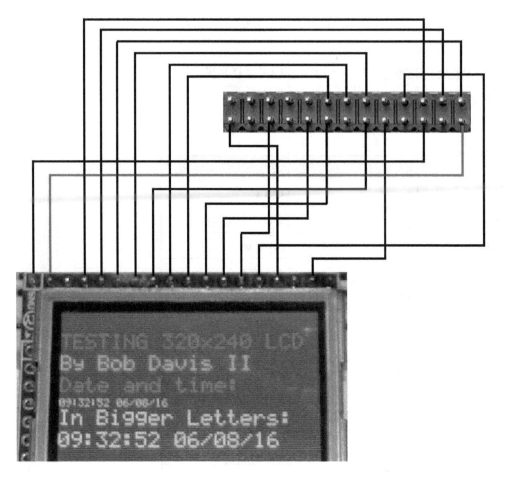

Here are some of the commands for the ILI9325.

No.	Registers Name	R/W	RS	D15	D14	D13	D12	D11	D10	D9	D8	D7	D6	D5	D4	D3	D2	D1	D0
IR	Index Register	W	0	-	-	-	-	-	-	-	-	ID7	ID6	ID5	ID4	ID3	ID2	ID1	ID0
00h	Driver Code Read	RO	1	1	0	0	1	0	0	1	1	0	0	1	0	0	1	0	1
01h	Driver Output Control 1	W	1	0	0	0	0	0	SM	0	SS	0	0	0	0	0	0	0	0
02h	LCD Driving Control	W	1	0	0	0	0	0	0	BC0	EOR	0	0	0	0	0	0	0	0
03h	Entry Mode	W	1	TRI	DFM	0	BGR	0	0	0	0	ORG	0	I/D1	I/D0	AM	0	0	0

Especially important is the last command "03".
When BGR is set is will swap the R and B order for writing data.
When TRI is set data is transferred to the RAM in 8-bit x 3 transfers.
DFM needs a chart to show how it sets up the color transfers.

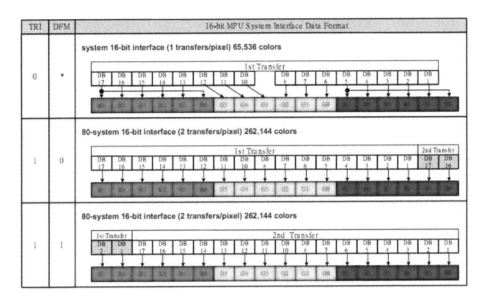

TRI	DFM	16-bit MPU System Interface Data Format

Coming up next is the code to make it work. Sorry the program is so long. There are two parallel output routines, one for commands, one for data. There are two text routines one for normal sized text and one for quad sized text, and of course the analog and sketch routines.

```python
# ILI9325 PARALLEL driver in python
# By Bob Davis
# Adapted from code on the Internet

import RPi.GPIO as GPIO
import time
import sys
# dATA lines
D0=17
D1=18
D2=27
D3=22
D4=23
D5=24
D6=25
D7=4
# cOMMAND Lines
RS=3    # Data/Control
RST=15 # Reset
CS=7    # Chip Select
WR=2    # Write clock
# MCP3008 lines
GPIO.setmode(GPIO.BCM)
```

```python
GPIO.setup(8, GPIO.OUT)   # CE0
GPIO.setup(9, GPIO.IN)    # MISO
GPIO.setup(10, GPIO.OUT)  # MOSI
GPIO.setup(11, GPIO.OUT)  # Sclock

font = { #reduced set
  ' ': [0x00, 0x00, 0x00, 0x00, 0x00],
  '/': [0x20, 0x10, 0x08, 0x04, 0x02],
  '0': [0x3e, 0x51, 0x49, 0x45, 0x3e],
  '1': [0x00, 0x42, 0x7f, 0x40, 0x00],
  '2': [0x42, 0x61, 0x51, 0x49, 0x46],
  '3': [0x21, 0x41, 0x45, 0x4b, 0x31],
  '4': [0x18, 0x14, 0x12, 0x7f, 0x10],
  '5': [0x27, 0x45, 0x45, 0x45, 0x39],
  '6': [0x3c, 0x4a, 0x49, 0x49, 0x30],
  '7': [0x01, 0x71, 0x09, 0x05, 0x03],
  '8': [0x36, 0x49, 0x49, 0x49, 0x36],
  '9': [0x06, 0x49, 0x49, 0x29, 0x1e],
  ':': [0x00, 0x36, 0x36, 0x00, 0x00],
  'A': [0x7e, 0x11, 0x11, 0x11, 0x7e],
  'B': [0x7f, 0x49, 0x49, 0x49, 0x36],
  'C': [0x3e, 0x41, 0x41, 0x41, 0x22],
  'D': [0x7f, 0x41, 0x41, 0x22, 0x1c],
  'E': [0x7f, 0x49, 0x49, 0x49, 0x41],
  'F': [0x7f, 0x09, 0x09, 0x09, 0x01],
  'G': [0x3e, 0x41, 0x49, 0x49, 0x7a],
  'H': [0x7f, 0x08, 0x08, 0x08, 0x7f],
  'I': [0x00, 0x41, 0x7f, 0x41, 0x00],
  'J': [0x20, 0x40, 0x41, 0x3f, 0x01],
  'K': [0x7f, 0x08, 0x14, 0x22, 0x41],
  'L': [0x7f, 0x40, 0x40, 0x40, 0x40],
  'M': [0x7f, 0x02, 0x0c, 0x02, 0x7f],
  'N': [0x7f, 0x04, 0x08, 0x10, 0x7f],
  'O': [0x3e, 0x41, 0x41, 0x41, 0x3e],
  'P': [0x7f, 0x09, 0x09, 0x09, 0x06],
  'Q': [0x3e, 0x41, 0x51, 0x21, 0x5e],
  'R': [0x7f, 0x09, 0x19, 0x29, 0x46],
  'S': [0x46, 0x49, 0x49, 0x49, 0x31],
  'T': [0x01, 0x01, 0x7f, 0x01, 0x01],
  'U': [0x3f, 0x40, 0x40, 0x40, 0x3f],
  'V': [0x1f, 0x20, 0x40, 0x20, 0x1f],
  'W': [0x3f, 0x40, 0x38, 0x40, 0x3f],
  'X': [0x63, 0x14, 0x08, 0x14, 0x63],
  'Y': [0x07, 0x08, 0x70, 0x08, 0x07],
  'Z': [0x61, 0x51, 0x49, 0x45, 0x43],
  '[': [0x00, 0x7f, 0x41, 0x41, 0x00],
```

```
  '\\': [0x02, 0x04, 0x08, 0x10, 0x20],
}

def init():
  GPIO.setup (D0, GPIO.OUT)
  GPIO.setup (D1, GPIO.OUT)
  GPIO.setup (D2, GPIO.OUT)
  GPIO.setup (D3, GPIO.OUT)
  GPIO.setup (D4, GPIO.OUT)
  GPIO.setup (D5, GPIO.OUT)
  GPIO.setup (D6, GPIO.OUT)
  GPIO.setup (D7, GPIO.OUT)
  GPIO.setup (RS, GPIO.OUT)
  GPIO.setup (RST, GPIO.OUT)
  GPIO.setup (CS, GPIO.OUT)
  GPIO.setup (WR, GPIO.OUT)
  Reset()

# set up for ILI9325D:
  WriteCD(0xE5, 0x78, 0xF0); # set SRAM internal timing
  WriteCD(0x01, 0x01, 0x00); # set Driver Output Control
  WriteCD(0x02, 0x02, 0x00); # set 1 line inversion
  WriteCD(0x03, 0xC0, 0x30); # D0=Set 3 bytes per color
BGR=1.
  WriteCD(0x04, 0x00, 0x00); # Resize register
  WriteCD(0x08, 0x02, 0x07); # set the back porch and front
porch
  WriteCD(0x09, 0x00, 0x00); # set non-display area refresh
cycle ISC[3:0]
  WriteCD(0x0A, 0x00, 0x00); # FMARK function
  WriteCD(0x0C, 0x00, 0x00); # RGB interface setting
  WriteCD(0x0D, 0x00, 0x00); # Frame marker Position
  WriteCD(0x0F, 0x00, 0x00); # RGB interface polarity
  WriteCD(0x10, 0x00, 0x00); # SAP, BT[3:0], AP, DSTB, SLP,
STB
  WriteCD(0x11, 0x00, 0x07); # DC1[2:0], DC0[2:0], VC[2:0]
  WriteCD(0x12, 0x00, 0x00); # VREG1OUT voltage
  WriteCD(0x13, 0x00, 0x00); # VDV[4:0] for VCOM amplitude
  WriteCD(0x07, 0x00, 0x01);
  time.sleep ( 0.00001 )
  WriteCD(0x10, 0x16, 0x90); # SAP, BT[3:0], AP, DSTB, SLP,
STB
  WriteCD(0x11, 0x02, 0x27); #DC1[2:0],DC0[2:0], VC[2:0]
  time.sleep ( 0.00001 )
  WriteCD(0x12, 0x00, 0x0D); # 0012
  time.sleep ( 0.00001 )
```

```python
    WriteCD(0x13, 0x12, 0x00); # VDV[4:0] VCOM amplitude
    WriteCD(0x29, 0x00, 0x0A); # 04  VCM[5:0] for VCOMH
    WriteCD(0x2B, 0x00, 0x0D); # Set Frame Rate
    time.sleep ( 0.00001 )
    WriteCD(0x20, 0x00, 0x00); # GRAM horizontal Address
    WriteCD(0x21, 0x00, 0x00); # GRAM Vertical Address
    WriteCD(0x30, 0x00, 0x00); # Gamma Curve
    WriteCD(0x31, 0x04, 0x04);
    WriteCD(0x32, 0x00, 0x03);
    WriteCD(0x35, 0x04, 0x05);
    WriteCD(0x36, 0x08, 0x08);
    WriteCD(0x37, 0x04, 0x07);
    WriteCD(0x38, 0x03, 0x03);
    WriteCD(0x39, 0x07, 0x07);
    WriteCD(0x3C, 0x05, 0x04);
    WriteCD(0x3D, 0x08, 0x08);
    #----------------- Set GRAM area --------------#
    WriteCD(0x50, 0x00, 0x00); # Horiz GRAM Start Adx
    WriteCD(0x51, 0x00, 0xEF); # Horiz GRAM End Address
    WriteCD(0x52, 0x00, 0x00); # Vert GRAM Start Address
    WriteCD(0x53, 0x01, 0x3F); # Vert GRAM Start Address
    WriteCD(0x60, 0xA7, 0x00); # Gate Scan Line
    WriteCD(0x61, 0x00, 0x01); # NDL,VLE, REV
    WriteCD(0x6A, 0x00, 0x00); # set scrolling line
    #-------------- Partial Display Control --------#
    WriteCD(0x80, 0x00, 0x00);
    WriteCD(0x81, 0x00, 0x00);
    WriteCD(0x82, 0x00, 0x00);
    WriteCD(0x83, 0x00, 0x00);
    WriteCD(0x84, 0x00, 0x00);
    WriteCD(0x85, 0x00, 0x00);
    #-------------- Panel Control ------------------#
    WriteCD(0x90, 0x00, 0x10);
    WriteCD(0x92, 0x00, 0x00);
    WriteCD(0x07, 0x01, 0x33); # 262K color display ON

def Reset (): # Reset Display
  GPIO.output (RST, True )
  GPIO.output (RST, False )
  time.sleep ( 0.1 )
  GPIO.output (RST, True )
  time.sleep ( 0.1 )
  GPIO.output (CS, True )
  GPIO.output (WR, True )
  time.sleep ( 0.1 )
```

```python
def WriteCmd (cmd): # Write Command
  for x in range (0,2):
    if (x==0):ccmd=0x00
    else: ccmd=cmd
    GPIO.output (RS, False )  # Register Select = 0
    GPIO.output (CS, False )  # Chip Select = 0
    GPIO.output (D0, False )
    GPIO.output (D1, False )
    GPIO.output (D2, False )
    GPIO.output (D3, False )
    GPIO.output (D4, False )
    GPIO.output (D5, False )
    GPIO.output (D6, False )
    GPIO.output (D7, False )
    if (ccmd & 0x01): GPIO.output (D0, True)
    if (ccmd & 0x02): GPIO.output (D1, True)
    if (ccmd & 0x04): GPIO.output (D2, True)
    if (ccmd & 0x08): GPIO.output (D3, True)
    if (ccmd & 0x10): GPIO.output (D4, True)
    if (ccmd & 0x20): GPIO.output (D5, True)
    if (ccmd & 0x40): GPIO.output (D6, True)
    if (ccmd & 0x80): GPIO.output (D7, True)
    GPIO.output (WR, False )
    GPIO.output (WR, True )  # write the data

def WriteData (cmd): # Write data
    data=cmd
    GPIO.output (RS, True )  # Register Select = 1
    GPIO.output (CS, False )  # Chip Select = 0
    GPIO.output (D0, False )
    GPIO.output (D1, False )
    GPIO.output (D2, False )
    GPIO.output (D3, False )
    GPIO.output (D4, False )
    GPIO.output (D5, False )
    GPIO.output (D6, False )
    GPIO.output (D7, False )
    if (data & 0x01): CPIO.output (D0, True)
    if (data & 0x02): GPIO.output (D1, True)
    if (data & 0x04): GPIO.output (D2, True)
    if (data & 0x08): GPIO.output (D3, True)
    if (data & 0x10): GPIO.output (D4, True)
    if (data & 0x20): GPIO.output (D5, True)
    if (data & 0x40): GPIO.output (D6, True)
    if (data & 0x80): GPIO.output (D7, True)
    GPIO.output (WR, False )
```

```
        GPIO.output (WR, True )   # write the data

def WriteCD (cmd,data1, data2): #Write command followed by
data
    WriteCmd (cmd )
    WriteData (data1)
    WriteData (data2)

def WriteMdata (mdata): #Write multiple data
  for index in range (len(mdata)):
    WriteData (mdata [index])

def Fill (red, green, blue, lines):
  if (red==1):red=255
  if (green==1):green=255
  if (blue==1):blue=255
  pixline = []
  for n in range (240): # Fill screen with color
    pixline.append (blue) # Blue
    pixline.append (green) # Green
    pixline.append (red) # Red
  for n in range (lines):    # 80=one quarter of LCD
    WriteMdata (pixline)

def goto (x, y):  # go to top/bottom
  WriteCD(0x20, 0x00, x); # GRAM horizontal Address
  if (y > 255):WriteCD(0x21, 0x01, y); # GRAM Vert Adx
  else: WriteCD(0x21, 0x00, y); # GRAM Vert Address
  WriteCmd ( 0X22 ) # Next: red, Green, Blue bytes

def Image (filename):
#  WriteCmd ( 0X22 ) # Next: red, Green, Blue bytes
  try:  # Prevents crashing when images do not work
    with open(filename, 'rb') as bitmap: # 240x320 image
      for x in range ( 0,320 ):
        pixline = []
        for y in range ( 0,720 ): # 720=3x240
#          bitmap.seek(0x36 + x*720 + (719-y)) # 36=header
          bitmap.seek(0x36 + (320-x)*720 + (y)) # flipped
          Pixel = ord(bitmap.read(1))
          pixline.append (Pixel)
        WriteMdata (pixline)
  except:
    pass

def text(string, red, green, blue):
```

```
#  WriteCmd ( 0X22 ) # Next: red, Green, Blue bytes
   string=string.ljust(40, " ") # 240/6=40 characters
   if (red==1):red=255
   if (green==1):green=255
   if (blue==1):blue=255
   string=string.ljust(40, " ") # 240/6=40 characters
   for row in range(0,10): # 10 rows top to bottom
     pixline = []
     for char in string: # Process each character
       for byte in range(0,5):
         data=(font[char])  # Load 5 bytes of character
         pix=0
         if (row<8):
           if(data[byte]>>row & 0x01):pix=1
         if (row>7):pix=0  # Blank between lines
         if (pix==1):       # fill in R/G/B
           pixline.append (blue)
           pixline.append (green)
           pixline.append (red)
         else:
           pixline.append (0x00)
           pixline.append (0x00)
           pixline.append (0x00)
     pixline.append (0x00) # blanks btw characters
     pixline.append (0x00)
     pixline.append (0x00)
   WriteMdata (pixline)
   pixline = []

def dtext(string, red, green, blue): # double size
   if (red==1):red=255
   if (green==1):green=255
   if (blue==1):blue=255
   string=string.ljust(20, " ") # 240/6=40 characters
   for row in range(0,20): # 20 rows top to bottom
     pixline = []
     for char in string: # Process each character
       for byte in range(0,5):
         data=(font[char])  # Load 5 bytes of character
         pix=0
         if (row<17):
           if(data[byte]>>(row/2) & 0x01):pix=1
         if (row>16):pix=0  # Blank between lines
         for twice in range(0,2):
           if (pix==1):        # fill in R/G/B
             pixline.append (blue)
```

```python
            pixline.append (green)
            pixline.append (red)
          else:
            pixline.append (0x00)
            pixline.append (0x00)
            pixline.append (0x00)
      for i in range(0,6):
          pixline.append (0x00) # blanks between characters
      WriteMdata (pixline)
      pixline = []

def readport(port):
  GPIO.output(8, GPIO.HIGH) # deselect chip
  GPIO.output(11, GPIO.LOW) # set clock low
  adcin=0
  for shift in range (0,24): # 24 pits shifted
    GPIO.output(8, GPIO.LOW) # select chip
    GPIO.output(10, GPIO.LOW) # low for most bits
    if (shift==7 or shift==8):
      GPIO.output(10, GPIO.HIGH)
    if (shift==9)and(port & 0x04):
      GPIO.output(10, GPIO.HIGH)
    if (shift==10)and(port & 0x02):
      GPIO.output(10, GPIO.HIGH)
    if (shift==11)and(port & 0x01):
      GPIO.output(10, GPIO.HIGH)
    if (shift > 13)and(GPIO.input(9)):
      adcin = adcin+1 # set bit
    adcin = adcin << 1  # left shift 1
    GPIO.output(11, GPIO.LOW) # cycle the clock
    GPIO.output(11, GPIO.HIGH)
#  print adcin
  return (adcin)

def sketch():
  for y in range(0,10000):
    pixline=[]
    analogx=(readport(0)/4)
    analogy=(readport(1)/4)
    analogr=(readport(5)/4)
    analogg=(readport(6)/4)
    analogb=(readport(7)/4)
    if analogx>239:analogx=239
    if analogy>239:analogy=239
    goto (analogx, analogy)
    WriteCmd (0X22) # Next: RGB bytes
```

```python
    pixline.append (analogr)
    pixline.append (analogg)
    pixline.append (analogb)
    WriteMdata (pixline)
    time.sleep(.01)

def scope():
  for x in range(0,320):
    pixline=[]
    alist=(readport(3)/4)
    goto (alist,x)#turned sideways
    WriteCmd (0X22) # Next: RGB bytes
    pixline.append (0xff)
    pixline.append (0xff)
    pixline.append (0xff)
    WriteMdata (pixline)

if __name__ == "__main__" :
  init ()
  goto (0, 64)
  Fill (1,0,0,64) # Blue
  goto (0, 128)
  Fill (0,1,0,64) # Green
  goto (0, 192)
  Fill (0,0,1,64) # Red
  goto (0, 256)
  Fill (1,1,1,64) # white
  time.sleep(2)

  goto(0,0)
  Image ("Parrots-240.bmp")
  time.sleep(2)

  goto(0,0)
  Fill (0,0,0,320) # black
  scope()
  time.sleep(2)

  goto(0,0)
  Fill (0,0,0,320) # black
  sketch()  #Convert time and date to strings
  time.sleep(2)

  goto(0,0)
  Fill (0,0,0,320) # black
  times=time.strftime('%H:%M:%S')
```

```
dates=time.strftime('%D')
# Read analog ports
analog1=(readport(0))   # Range 0-1024
analog2=(readport(1))
analog3=(readport(2))
analog4=(readport(3))
analog5=(readport(4))
analog6=(readport(5))
analog7=(readport(6))
analog8=(readport(7))
text("THIS IS A TEST OF THE 320X240 LCD", 1,0,0) # Blue
text("WRITTEN BY ROBERT J DAVIS II", 0,1,0)  # green
text("THE CURRENT DATE AND TIME IS:", 0,0,1) # RED
text(times+" "+dates, 1,1,1)     # white
dtext ("IN BIGGER LETTERS:", 1,0,1)
dtext(times+" "+dates, 1,1,1)     # white
text("ANALOG 1 IS "+str(analog1),1,1,1)
text("ANALOG 2 IS "+str(analog2),1,1,0)
text("ANALOG 3 IS "+str(analog3),0,1,1)
text("ANALOG 4 IS "+str(analog4),1,0,1)
text("ANALOG 5 IS "+str(analog5),1,1,1)
text("ANALOG 6 IS "+str(analog6),1,1,0)
text("ANALOG 7 IS "+str(analog7),0,1,1)
text("ANALOG 8 IS "+str(analog8),1,0,1)
print 'Done'
```

Chapter 10

3.2 inch TFT Parallel 240x320

This LCD screen was designed for 16 bit operations. That would require the use of shift registers to get the needed 16 bits of data. However by reading the instruction manuals for the LCD's it became obvious that the manufacturers make them capable of multiple modes of operation. The trick is to figure out how to modify the LCD.

After unsnapping the metal catches with a knife the display flips up revealing the ribbon cable that connects it to the circuit board. On that ribbon cable there are marking for R1 and R2 but only r2 is present.

Use a box cutter knife to cut the solder at the bottom end of R2 and then flip the resistor up breaking the top connection. Then take a small stranded wire and separate out one strand. Lay that strand across the R1 contacts. Tap it with a soldering iron and it should instantly be soldered in place. Cut off the rest of the wire. My soldering iron tip deposited some solder on the unused pins to the left.

With this change I thought the adapter that worked with the previous LCD's would work. That was a big mistake. After days of trying the solution was found in the SSd1289 manual. The previous LCD's used D8 to D15 as D0 to D7 when in the 8 bit mode. The SSD1289 does not do that. It uses Do-D7 as their name sakes, but they are found on the second row of pins. The only way to access the second row is to adapt one of the adapters or make a new one.

This is the wiring chart this time the LCD pins are not completely in order because DB0 to DB7 are located on the second row of pins.

LCD pins	Raspberry Pi Pins	Pi Pin Name
Gnd	6	Gnd
VCC	2	+5V
NC		
RS	5	SCL
RW	3	SDA
RD	1	+3V (Disabled)

DB8	NC	
DB9	NC	
DB10	NC	
DB11	NC	
DB12	NC	
DB13	NC	
DB14	NC	
DB15	NC	
CS	26	CE1
NC		
Reset	10	RX
NC		
LED A	1	+3V
NC		
Second Row of Pins		
DB0	11	GPIO0
DB1	12	GPIO1
DB2	13	GPIO2
DB3	15	GPIO3
DB4	16	GPIO4
DB5	18	GPIO5
DB6	22	GPIO6
DB7	7	GPIO7

Coming up next is the schematic diagram. This time the LCD connector is shown from the bottom view. I used a flexible ribbon cable so the LCD can be flipped over after it is connected up.

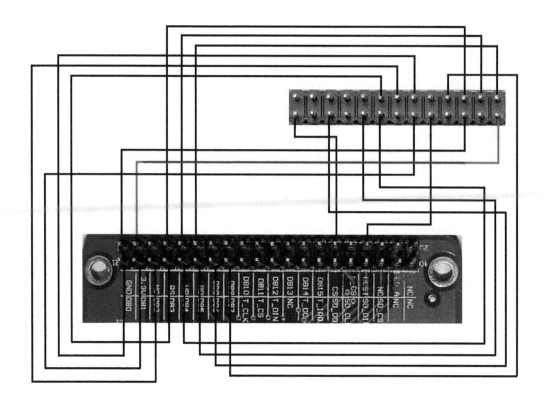

There are two registers that are changed from the standard code found on the Internet to get the LCD to work properly. Start with the register 01 settings chart shown below, several bits have no default settings.

Driver Output Control (R01h) (POR = |0XXXX0X1|3Fh)

R/W	DC	IB15	IB14	IB13	IB12	IB11	IB10	IB9	IB8	IB7	IB6	IB5	IB4	IB3	IB2	IB1	IB0
W	1	0	RL	REV	CAD	BGR	SM	TB	MUX8	MUX7	MUX6	MUX5	MUX4	MUX3	MUX2	MUX1	MUX0
POR		0	X	X	X	X	0	X	1	0	0	1	1	1	1	1	1

There are two settings that need to be modified here:
When BGR = "0" <R><G><B> color is assigned from S0.
When BGR = "1" <B><G><R> color is assigned from S0.
When RL = "1", S0 shifts to S719 (Needed so graphics are correct)
When RL = "0", S719 shifts to S0

Here is the register 11 settings chart, the bottom row is the default settings.

Entry Mode (R11h) (POR = 6830h)

R/W	DC	IB15	IB14	IB13	IB12	IB11	IB10	IB9	IB8	IB7	IB6	IB5	IB4	IB3	IB2	IB1	IB0
W	1	VSMode	DFM1	DFM0	TRANS	OEDef	WMode	DMode1	DMode0	TY1	TY0	ID1	ID0	AM	LG2	LG1	LG0
POR		0	1	1	0	1	0	0	0	0	0	1	1	0	0	0	0

The DFM setting is critical as it sets the color mode according to this chart
DFM1 DFM0 Color mode

| ---- | ---- | ------------- |
| 1 | 1 | 65k color (Default Setting) |
| 1 | 0 | 262k color (Needed for BMP graphics) |

Here is the code to make it work. The sketch has been improved so you can select the color with switches. You could also use variable resistors to give infinite colors.

```python
# SSD1289 PARALLEL driver in python
# By Bob Davis
# Parts are from code on the Internet

import RPi.GPIO as GPIO
import time
import sys
# dATA lines
D0=17
D1=18
D2=27
D3=22
D4=23
D5=24
D6=25
D7=4
# cOMMAND Lines
RS=3   # Data/Control
RST=15 # Reset
CS=7   # Chip Select
WR=2   # Write clock
# MCP3008 lines
GPIO.setmode(GPIO.BCM)
GPIO.setup(8, GPIO.OUT)   # CE0
GPIO.setup(9, GPIO.IN)    # MISO
GPIO.setup(10, GPIO.OUT)  # MOSI
GPIO.setup(11, GPIO.OUT)  # Sclock

font = [
    ' ': [0x00, 0x00, 0x00, 0x00, 0x00],
    '!': [0x00, 0x00, 0x5f, 0x00, 0x00],
    '"': [0x00, 0x07, 0x00, 0x07, 0x00],
    '#': [0x14, 0x7f, 0x14, 0x7f, 0x14],
    '$': [0x24, 0x2a, 0x7f, 0x2a, 0x12],
    '%': [0x23, 0x13, 0x08, 0x64, 0x62],
    '&': [0x36, 0x49, 0x55, 0x22, 0x50],
    "'": [0x00, 0x05, 0x03, 0x00, 0x00],
    '(': [0x00, 0x1c, 0x22, 0x41, 0x00],
```

```
')': [0x00, 0x41, 0x22, 0x1c, 0x00],
'*': [0x14, 0x08, 0x3e, 0x08, 0x14],
'+': [0x08, 0x08, 0x3e, 0x08, 0x08],
',': [0x00, 0x50, 0x30, 0x00, 0x00],
'-': [0x08, 0x08, 0x08, 0x08, 0x08],
'.': [0x00, 0x60, 0x60, 0x00, 0x00],
'/': [0x20, 0x10, 0x08, 0x04, 0x02],
'0': [0x3e, 0x51, 0x49, 0x45, 0x3e],
'1': [0x00, 0x42, 0x7f, 0x40, 0x00],
'2': [0x42, 0x61, 0x51, 0x49, 0x46],
'3': [0x21, 0x41, 0x45, 0x4b, 0x31],
'4': [0x18, 0x14, 0x12, 0x7f, 0x10],
'5': [0x27, 0x45, 0x45, 0x45, 0x39],
'6': [0x3c, 0x4a, 0x49, 0x49, 0x30],
'7': [0x01, 0x71, 0x09, 0x05, 0x03],
'8': [0x36, 0x49, 0x49, 0x49, 0x36],
'9': [0x06, 0x49, 0x49, 0x29, 0x1e],
':': [0x00, 0x36, 0x36, 0x00, 0x00],
';': [0x00, 0x56, 0x36, 0x00, 0x00],
'<': [0x08, 0x14, 0x22, 0x41, 0x00],
'=': [0x14, 0x14, 0x14, 0x14, 0x14],
'>': [0x00, 0x41, 0x22, 0x14, 0x08],
'?': [0x02, 0x01, 0x51, 0x09, 0x06],
'@': [0x32, 0x49, 0x79, 0x41, 0x3e],
'A': [0x7e, 0x11, 0x11, 0x11, 0x7e],
'B': [0x7f, 0x49, 0x49, 0x49, 0x36],
'C': [0x3e, 0x41, 0x41, 0x41, 0x22],
'D': [0x7f, 0x41, 0x41, 0x22, 0x1c],
'E': [0x7f, 0x49, 0x49, 0x49, 0x41],
'F': [0x7f, 0x09, 0x09, 0x09, 0x01],
'G': [0x3e, 0x41, 0x49, 0x49, 0x7a],
'H': [0x7f, 0x08, 0x08, 0x08, 0x7f],
'I': [0x00, 0x41, 0x7f, 0x41, 0x00],
'J': [0x20, 0x40, 0x41, 0x3f, 0x01],
'K': [0x7f, 0x08, 0x14, 0x22, 0x41],
'L': [0x7f, 0x40, 0x40, 0x40, 0x40],
'M': [0x7f, 0x02, 0x0c, 0x02, 0x7f],
'N': [0x7f, 0x04, 0x08, 0x10, 0x7f],
'O': [0x3e, 0x41, 0x41, 0x41, 0x3e],
'P': [0x7f, 0x09, 0x09, 0x09, 0x06],
'Q': [0x3e, 0x41, 0x51, 0x21, 0x5e],
'R': [0x7f, 0x09, 0x19, 0x29, 0x46],
'S': [0x46, 0x49, 0x49, 0x49, 0x31],
'T': [0x01, 0x01, 0x7f, 0x01, 0x01],
'U': [0x3f, 0x40, 0x40, 0x40, 0x3f],
'V': [0x1f, 0x20, 0x40, 0x20, 0x1f],
'W': [0x3f, 0x40, 0x38, 0x40, 0x3f],
'X': [0x63, 0x14, 0x08, 0x14, 0x63],
'Y': [0x07, 0x08, 0x70, 0x08, 0x07],
'Z': [0x61, 0x51, 0x49, 0x45, 0x43],
```

```python
    '[': [0x00, 0x7f, 0x41, 0x41, 0x00],
    '\\': [0x02, 0x04, 0x08, 0x10, 0x20],
    ']': [0x00, 0x41, 0x41, 0x7f, 0x00],
    '^': [0x04, 0x02, 0x01, 0x02, 0x04],
    '_': [0x40, 0x40, 0x40, 0x40, 0x40],
    '`': [0x00, 0x01, 0x02, 0x04, 0x00],
    'a': [0x20, 0x54, 0x54, 0x54, 0x78],
    'b': [0x7f, 0x48, 0x44, 0x44, 0x38],
    'c': [0x38, 0x44, 0x44, 0x44, 0x20],
    'd': [0x38, 0x44, 0x44, 0x48, 0x7f],
    'e': [0x38, 0x54, 0x54, 0x54, 0x18],
    'f': [0x08, 0x7e, 0x09, 0x01, 0x02],
    'g': [0x0c, 0x52, 0x52, 0x52, 0x3e],
    'h': [0x7f, 0x08, 0x04, 0x04, 0x78],
    'i': [0x00, 0x44, 0x7d, 0x40, 0x00],
    'j': [0x20, 0x40, 0x44, 0x3d, 0x00],
    'k': [0x7f, 0x10, 0x28, 0x44, 0x00],
    'l': [0x00, 0x41, 0x7f, 0x40, 0x00],
    'm': [0x7c, 0x04, 0x18, 0x04, 0x78],
    'n': [0x7c, 0x08, 0x04, 0x04, 0x78],
    'o': [0x38, 0x44, 0x44, 0x44, 0x38],
    'p': [0x7c, 0x14, 0x14, 0x14, 0x08],
    'q': [0x08, 0x14, 0x14, 0x18, 0x7c],
    'r': [0x7c, 0x08, 0x04, 0x04, 0x08],
    's': [0x48, 0x54, 0x54, 0x54, 0x20],
    't': [0x04, 0x3f, 0x44, 0x40, 0x20],
    'u': [0x3c, 0x40, 0x40, 0x20, 0x7c],
    'v': [0x1c, 0x20, 0x40, 0x20, 0x1c],
    'w': [0x3c, 0x40, 0x30, 0x40, 0x3c],
    'x': [0x44, 0x28, 0x10, 0x28, 0x44],
    'y': [0x0c, 0x50, 0x50, 0x50, 0x3c],
    'z': [0x44, 0x64, 0x54, 0x4c, 0x44],
    '{': [0x00, 0x08, 0x36, 0x41, 0x00],
    '|': [0x00, 0x00, 0x7f, 0x00, 0x00],
    '}': [0x00, 0x41, 0x36, 0x08, 0x00],
    '~': [0x10, 0x08, 0x08, 0x10, 0x08],
}

def init():
  GPIO.setup (D0, GPIO.OUT)
  GPIO.setup (D1, GPIO.OUT)
  GPIO.setup (D2, GPIO.OUT)
  GPIO.setup (D3, GPIO.OUT)
  GPIO.setup (D4, GPIO.OUT)
  GPIO.setup (D5, GPIO.OUT)
  GPIO.setup (D6, GPIO.OUT)
  GPIO.setup (D7, GPIO.OUT)
  GPIO.setup (RS, GPIO.OUT)
  GPIO.setup (RST, GPIO.OUT)
  GPIO.setup (CS, GPIO.OUT)
```

```
    GPIO.setup (WR, GPIO.OUT)
    Reset()

# set up for SSD1289:
    WriteCD(0x00, 0x00, 0x01);
    WriteCD(0x03, 0xA8, 0xA4);
    WriteCD(0x0C, 0x00, 0x00);
    WriteCD(0x0D, 0x08, 0x0C);
    WriteCD(0x0E, 0x2B, 0x00);
    WriteCD(0x1E, 0x00, 0xB7);
    WriteCD(0x01, 0x61, 0x3f);
    WriteCD(0x02, 0x06, 0x00);
    WriteCD(0x10, 0x00, 0x00);
    WriteCD(0x11, 0x48, 0x30);  # 3 bytes per color
    WriteCD(0x05, 0x00, 0x00);
    WriteCD(0x06, 0x00, 0x00);
    WriteCD(0x16, 0xEF, 0x1C);
    WriteCD(0x17, 0x00, 0x03);
    WriteCD(0x07, 0x02, 0x33);
    WriteCD(0x0B, 0x00, 0x00);
    WriteCD(0x0F, 0x00, 0x00);
    WriteCD(0x41, 0x00, 0x00);
    WriteCD(0x42, 0x00, 0x00);
    WriteCD(0x48, 0x00, 0x00);
    WriteCD(0x49, 0x01, 0x3F);
    WriteCD(0x4A, 0x00, 0x00);
    WriteCD(0x4B, 0x00, 0x00);
    WriteCD(0x44, 0xEF, 0x00);
    WriteCD(0x45, 0x00, 0x00);
    WriteCD(0x46, 0x01, 0x3F);
    WriteCD(0x23, 0x00, 0x00);
    WriteCD(0x24, 0x00, 0x00);
    WriteCD(0x25, 0x80, 0x00);
    WriteCD(0x4f, 0x00, 0x00);  # X position
    WriteCD(0x4e, 0x00, 0x00);  # Y Position
#   WriteCmd(0x22);

def Reset (): # Reset Display
    GPIO.output (RST, True )
    GPIO.output (RST, False )
    time.sleep ( 0.1 )
    GPIO.output (RST, True )
    time.sleep ( 0.1 )
    GPIO.output (CS, True )
    GPIO.output (WR, True )
    time.sleep ( 0.1 )

def WriteCmd (cmd): # Write Command
    for x in range (0,2):
        if (x==0):ccmd=0x00
```

```
        else: ccmd=cmd
        ccmd=cmd
        GPIO.output (RS, False )  # Register Select = 0
        GPIO.output (CS, False )  # Chip Select = 0
        GPIO.output (D0, False )
        GPIO.output (D1, False )
        GPIO.output (D2, False )
        GPIO.output (D3, False )
        GPIO.output (D4, False )
        GPIO.output (D5, False )
        GPIO.output (D6, False )
        GPIO.output (D7, False )
        if (ccmd & 0x01): GPIO.output (D0, True)
        if (ccmd & 0x02): GPIO.output (D1, True)
        if (ccmd & 0x04): GPIO.output (D2, True)
        if (ccmd & 0x08): GPIO.output (D3, True)
        if (ccmd & 0x10): GPIO.output (D4, True)
        if (ccmd & 0x20): GPIO.output (D5, True)
        if (ccmd & 0x40): GPIO.output (D6, True)
        if (ccmd & 0x80): GPIO.output (D7, True)
        GPIO.output (WR, False )
#       time.sleep ( tdelay )
        GPIO.output (WR, True )  # write the data
        GPIO.output (CS, True )  # Chip Select = 1

def WriteData (cmd): # Write data
        data=cmd
        GPIO.output (RS, True )  # Register Select = 1
        GPIO.output (CS, False )  # Chip Select = 0
        GPIO.output (D0, False )
        GPIO.output (D1, False )
        GPIO.output (D2, False )
        GPIO.output (D3, False )
        GPIO.output (D4, False )
        GPIO.output (D5, False )
        GPIO.output (D6, False )
        GPIO.output (D7, False )
        if (data & 0x01): GPIO.output (D0, True)
        if (data & 0x02): GPIO.output (D1, True)
        if (data & 0x04): GPIO.output (D2, True)
        if (data & 0x08): GPIO.output (D3, True)
        if (data & 0x10): CPIO.output (D4, True)
        if (data & 0x20): GPIO.output (D5, True)
        if (data & 0x40): GPIO.output (D6, True)
        if (data & 0x80): GPIO.output (D7, True)
        GPIO.output (WR, False )
#       time.sleep ( tdelay )
        GPIO.output (WR, True )  # write the data
        GPIO.output (CS, True )  # Chip Select = 1
```

```python
def WriteCD (cmd,data1, data2): #Write command followed by data
    WriteCmd (cmd )
    WriteData (data1)
    WriteData (data2)

def WriteMdata (mdata): #Write multiple data
  for index in range (len(mdata)):
    WriteData (mdata [index])

def Fill (red, green, blue):
  WriteCmd ( 0X22 ) # Next: red, Green, Blue bytes
  pixline = []
  for n in range (240): # Fill screen with color
    if (blue==1):pixline.append (0xffff) # Blue
    else :pixline.append (0x0000) # Blue
    if (green==1):pixline.append (0xffff) # Green
    else :pixline.append (0x0000) # Green
    if (red==1):pixline.append (0xffff) # RED
    else: pixline.append (0x0000) # RED
  for n in range (320):    # 80=one quarter of LCD
    WriteMdata (pixline)

def goto (x, y):  # go to top/bottom
  WriteCD(0x4f, 0x00, x); # GRAM horizontal Address
  WriteCD(0x4e, 0x00, y); # GRAM Vertical Address

def Image (filename):
  WriteCmd ( 0X22 ) # Next: red, Green, Blue bytes
  try:  # Prevents crashing when images do not work
    with open(filename, 'rb') as bitmap: # Must be 128x128
      for x in range ( 0,320 ):
        pixline = []
        for y in range ( 0,720 ): # 720=3x240
#           bitmap.seek(0x36 + x*720 + (719-y)) # 36=header
          bitmap.seek(0x36 + (320-x)*720 + (y)) # flipped
          Pixel = ord(bitmap.read(1))
          pixline.append (Pixel)
        WriteMdata (pixline)
  except:
      pass

def text(string, red, green, blue):
  WriteCmd ( 0X22 ) # Next: red, Green, Blue bytes
  string=string.ljust(40, " ") # 240/6=40 characters
  for row in range(10): # 10 rows top to bottom
    pixline = []
    for char in string: # Procees each character in string
      for byte in range(5):
        data=(font[char])  # Load 5 bytes of character
        pix=0
```

```python
        if (row==0) and (data[byte] & 0x01):pix=1
        if (row==1) and (data[byte] & 0x02):pix=1
        if (row==2) and (data[byte] & 0x04):pix=1
        if (row==3) and (data[byte] & 0x08):pix=1
        if (row==4) and (data[byte] & 0x10):pix=1
        if (row==5) and (data[byte] & 0x20):pix=1
        if (row==6) and (data[byte] & 0x40):pix=1
        if (row==7) and (data[byte] & 0x80):pix=1
        if (row==8):pix=0  # Blank between lines
        if (row==9):pix=0  # Blank between lines
        if (pix==1):        # fill in R/G/B
          if (blue==1): pixline.append (0xff)
          else: pixline.append (0x00)
          if (green==1): pixline.append (0xff)
          else: pixline.append (0x00)
          if (red==1): pixline.append (0xff)
          else: pixline.append (0x00)
        else:
            pixline.append (0x00)
            pixline.append (0x00)
            pixline.append (0x00)
      pixline.append (0x00) # blanks between characters
      pixline.append (0x00)
      pixline.append (0x00)
    WriteMdata (pixline)
    pixline = []

def dtext(string, red, green, blue): # double size text
  WriteCmd ( 0X22 ) # Next: red, Green, Blue bytes
  string=string.ljust(20, " ") # 240/6=40 characters
  for row in range(20): # 20 rows top to bottom
    pixline = []
    for char in string: # Procees each character in string
      for byte in range(5):
        data=(font[char])  # Load 5 bytes of character
        pix=0
        if ((row==0)or(row==1))and(data[byte]& 0x01):pix=1
        if ((row==2)or(row==3))and(data[byte]& 0x02):pix=1
        if ((row==4)or(row==5))and(data[byte]& 0x04):pix=1
        if ((row==6)or(row==7))and(data[byte]& 0x08):pix=1
        if ((row==8)or(row==9))and(data[byte]& 0x10):pix=1
        it ((row==10)or(row--11))and(data[byte]&0x20):pix=1
        if ((row==12)or(row==13))and(data[byte]&0x40):pix=1
        if ((row==14)or(row==15))and(data[byte]&0x80):pix=1
        if (row>16):pix=0  # Blank between lines
        for twice in range(2):
          if (pix==1):        # fill in R/G/B
            if (blue==1): pixline.append (0xff)
            else: pixline.append (0x00)
            if (green==1): pixline.append (0xff)
```

```
          else: pixline.append (0x00)
            if (red==1): pixline.append (0xff)
            else: pixline.append (0x00)
          else:
            pixline.append (0x00)
            pixline.append (0x00)
            pixline.append (0x00)
      for x in range (0,6):
        pixline.append (0x00) # blanks between characters
    WriteMdata (pixline)
    pixline = []

def readport(port):
  GPIO.output(8, GPIO.HIGH) # deselect chip
  GPIO.output(11, GPIO.LOW) # set clock low
  adcin=0
  for shift in range (0,24): # 24 pits shifted
    GPIO.output(8, GPIO.LOW) # select chip
    GPIO.output(10, GPIO.LOW) # low for most bits
    if (shift==7 or shift==8):
      GPIO.output(10, GPIO.HIGH)
    if (shift==9)and(port & 0x04):
      GPIO.output(10, GPIO.HIGH)
    if (shift==10)and(port & 0x02):
      GPIO.output(10, GPIO.HIGH)
    if (shift==11)and(port & 0x01):
      GPIO.output(10, GPIO.HIGH)
    if (shift > 13)and(GPIO.input(9)):
      adcin = adcin+1 # set bit
    adcin = adcin << 1  # left shift 1
    GPIO.output(11, GPIO.LOW) # cycle the clock
    GPIO.output(11, GPIO.HIGH)
#  print adcin
  return (adcin)

def sketch():
  for y in range(0,10000):
    pixline=[]
    analogx=(readport(0)/4)
    analogy=(readport(1)/4)
    analogr=(readport(5)/4)
    analogg=(readport(6)/4)
    analogb=(readport(7)/4)
    if analogx>239:analogx=239
    if analogy>239:analogy=239
    goto (analogx, analogy)
    WriteCmd ( 0X22 ) # Next: red, Green, Blue bytes
    pixline.append (analogr)
    pixline.append (analogg)
    pixline.append (analogb)
```

```python
        print (analogr)
        WriteMdata (pixline)
        time.sleep(.01)

if __name__ == "__main__" :
    init ()
    T1 = time.clock ()
    goto(0,0)
    Image ("Parrots-240.bmp")
    time.sleep(2)
    goto(0,0)
    #Convert time and date to strings
    times=time.strftime('%H:%M:%S')
    dates=time.strftime('%D')
    dtext ("     ", 0,0,0)
    dtext("TESTING 320x240 LCD", 1,0,0) # Red
    dtext ("     ", 0,0,0)
    dtext("By Bob Davis II", 0,1,0)  # green
    dtext ("     ", 0,0,0)
    dtext("The date and time:", 0,0,1) # Blue
    dtext ("     ", 0,0,0)
    text(times+" "+dates, 1,1,1)    # white
    dtext ("     ", 0,0,0)
    dtext ("In Bigger Letters:", 1,1,1)
    dtext ("     ", 0,0,0)
    dtext(times+" "+dates, 1,1,1)    # white
    dtext ("     ", 0,0,0)
    dtext ("Etch-a-Sketch Next", 1,1,1)
    dtext ("     ", 0,0,0)
    time.sleep(2)
    goto(0,0)
    Fill (0,0,0) # black
    time.sleep(2)
    sketch()

    T2 = time.clock ()
    print 'Processing Time:' , str (T2 - T1)
# End
```

Bibliography

These are some of the books that I used in writing this book.

Raspberry Pi
A Quick-Start Guide
Maik Schmidt
The Pragmatic Bookshelf
Dallas, Texas • Raleigh, North Carolina
Copyright © 2012 The Pragmatic Programmers, LLC.

Python Tutorial
Simply Easy Learning by tutorialspoint.com
Copyright © tutorialspoint.com

Raspberry Pi Cookbook
by Simon Monk
Copyright © 2014 Simon Monk. All rights reserved.

Here are some really great web sites:

This web site is a tremendous resource for the Raspberry Pi.
http://www.raspberrypi.org/

Adafruit has a special section for the Raspberry Pi.
https://learn.adafruit.com/category/raspberry-pi

There are many free magazines that you can download.
http://www.themagpi.com/issues/